GARDEN COLOUR SERIES

SHRUBS AND SMALL TREES

David Stuart

AURA
EDITIONS

Endpapers *The finest of the lacecap hydrangeas,* H. macrophylla *'Blue Wave'.*
Title page *Ceanothus* 'Gloire de Versailles' *flowers in late summer, given full sun and good soil.*
Right *A bed of dwarf rhododendrons, heathers and conifers will provide colour and interest all year round.*

Series Editor: Susan Conder
Editor: Eluned James
Art Editor: Caroline Dewing

Published by
Aura Editions
2 Derby Road
Greenford, Middlesex

Produced by Marshall Cavendish Books Ltd
58 Old Compton Street
London W1V 5PA

ISBN 0 86307 273 9

Typeset in Ehrhardt 453 by Walkergate Press, Anlaby
Printed and bound in Hong Kong by Dai Nippon
Printing Company

CONTENTS

INTRODUCTION

INTRODUCTION

The addition of well chosen shrubs and trees will be an integral part of most garden schemes and, by following a few basic guide-lines, costly errors can easily be avoided.

If you've just taken on a new garden, or want to change the one you have, you're in a fortunate position. Whatever size it is, whether an acre in the country, or a tiny and shaded courtyard in the inner city, you can accommodate lovely trees and shrubs. You can have somewhere nice to sit in summer, serene and leafy if you want that, or a blaze of colour if you prefer, somewhere to potter about in spring and autumn, and to watch or work in during the winter.

However small your garden, however overlooked, however difficult the shape or the soil, with a bit of thought, and the help of your plants you can have a space that will delight both you and others. There are a few basic points, though.

Don't be in too much of a hurry. The more 'difficult' your garden, the more consideration it needs, both as to what you actually want from it, what it can give, and what trees and shrubs will grow. Most new gardeners want, understandably, 'instant' gardens, and so plant fast growing subjects, or anything which is in flower at the garden centre. This can lead both to lost opportunities, and expensive mistakes. So stop and consider.

Every gardener and every garden is unique. The garden is there to do what you want it to do – so think about what you want. It's easy to accept conventional ideas about what makes a 'good' garden – but do you actually want a rockery? Do you really want a blaze of colour all the year round? Isn't an infinite series of greens just as good? Is a heather garden really a good idea? Do you actually like heathers? Is 'low maintenance' important, when gardening can be immense fun and very satisfying?

Once you've decided, there are one or two easy-to-remember things that will help the final results look good. Most people are quite greedy, and gardeners are no different. However, try to keep things simple. If you don't like dwarf conifers, but you do like yellow roses, fill the whole garden with different sorts of yellow rose (try planting them with ferns, variegated hostas, periwinkles, and have a few pots of carmine pink petunias for contrast). If you like flowering cherries, plant a dozen of the same type – there are many plants you could grow underneath – and if you have window boxes, plant them all the same way.

Brilliant colours can look wonderful set against plenty of gentle greenery to cool them down. If you really do want sheets of colour (and plenty of plants will give you just that), you'll find that the softer the colours, the more easily and elegantly they combine. Use brilliant colours for occasional 'accents'.

Garden maintenance is always a problem. Lots of gardeners opt for low maintenance plants not because they're so enormously busy, but because they're not sure about pruning, training, pests, and so on. Absolutely none of these is a real difficulty – almost no-one would garden if they were. Even worse, almost every low maintenance solution to planting gardens eventually becomes boring – partly because it really is never changing, partly because it demands no involvement on the gardener's part. There isn't any reason why even a tiny garden should bore you. The following chapters describe only a tiny portion of the trees and shrubs you could grow, and yet they still include plants to give you flowers and perfume in deepest winter (or even attractive winter stems) – and all sorts of good things to look at in the other seasons.

Of course, gardening isn't all plants, though there are often 'garden' solutions to other garden problems. If you want to eat outdoors and in shade, rather than buy an umbrella, why not build a small pergola against a wall, where you can dine in the shade of vines, roses and jasmine? Rather than expensive seating, at least consider a turf bank – a medieval idea, wonderfully comfortable and damp only after heavy rains. If parts of your garden are too shady for grass, why not try some of the many lovely ivies available, as a cheaper substitute for concrete slabs?

You'll find that garden accessories often look 'right' if they're made of natural materials. Folding chairs of wood and canvas often look better than alloy and floral nylon ones; a simple earthenware pot soon looks better than a curly white plastic urn. Wooden benches, even if white painted, often look better than fancy white-coated aluminium ones. Unfortunately, natural materials are often more expensive than modern ones, but they do age and mature – developing an atmosphere of their own. And in a pretty garden, atmosphere is all.

Opposite Skimmia japonica *is an excellent ground-cover shrub for shade and moist soil and will berry freely if planted in groups of male and female plants. Generally, birds leave the berries alone, so they can be enjoyed for a long period.*

CHAPTER 1

BUYING AND CARING FOR SHRUBS

To get the most benefit and long-term pleasure from shrubs and trees, it is important to start off with healthy plants and exactly the right selection of plants for your particular garden.

Before you buy plants for your garden, it's always worth deciding in advance where your new purchase is going to go. A good motto is 'Know your garden': that way, you'll know which parts are always in shade, which parts get baked by the sun, which parts are wind tunnels, which are damp or dry, and which have good or bad soil.

There are always quite a few plants which will grow in almost any combination of these conditions, but only very few that will grow happily in all of them. If you're going to get the best value from the plants you buy, you'll need to match the plants' requirements with the sorts of environment you can offer.

Most of the plants described in the following chapters have strong constitutions, but even they will only give of their best if you can give them their favourite conditions. However, there are thousands and thousands of garden plants, and some of these can be finicky indeed. Garden centre plants often have informative labels, so always have a quick look at those before you buy. If you're buying from a nursery, always ask the sales assistant what the plant likes or dislikes.

If you're in the fortunate position of planning and planting a new garden, it's always tempting to write out a list of all the shrubs, trees and flowers that you like, then rush off and buy them. You'll probably find that, once you get them home, they all need to planted in perfect soil and in full sun.

Try to work from what you can offer your plants, and not put plants into places where they won't grow. That way, you'll soon have a lovely and luxuriant garden, full of colour and perfume, and one that will repay in full the little bit of extra research you've had to do at the start.

Where and when to buy
Plants are available from all sorts of sources – from the little nursery down the road, from chain stores, garden centres, right up to the glossy and famous nurseries that could stock a botanic garden. Good plants can be bought from all of these sources.

Don't, on the whole, buy mixed collections of shrubs advertised in newspapers. Some can be excellent, but others are simply surplus or unsaleable stock, put together with no thought of what will grow or look good in your own garden.

If you buy through mail-order firms, and you're not after anything rare, choose a large and reputable nursery. Almost all are exceptionally helpful if you run into any problems, and the material they send out is of good quality.

The only difficulty with mail order is that your plants will arrive during the winter, and will probably be 'bare rooted'. They need to be planted at once, and it's sometimes difficult to judge how they will look together.

If you're keen to buy containerized plants, you'll find a good range at most garden centres and more unusual plants at most nurseries.

Let mail-order nurseries know what you want as early as you can in autumn – that way, you ought to get everything you've asked for. Mail-order buying means winter work in the garden.

You can plant containerized plants as soon as you've got them home, but there's no rush. It's worth moving the new plants around a bit to see where they make the most impact, then plant them. Don't do this job, though, just before you go on holiday – they often need careful attention for the first month or two after planting.

What to look for when buying
Plant shape, leaves, flowers and even the weeds growing in the containers are all worth looking at – so the best time to visit garden centres is between late spring and late summer.

Shape If you're buying a tree, whether a full standard, or a half standard, look for a good, straight trunk, with undamaged bark, secured loosely but well to its support. The plant should have a good, open crown with

Opposite An old apple tree makes an excellent support for one of the ornamental ivies, which revels in the dappled shade and cool moist soil. The underplanting is formed with other shade-lovers: ferns and spurges.

If bare-rooted shrubs and trees cannot be planted immediately on arrival, perhaps due to frozen or very wet soil, they can be temporarily heeled-in, in a sheltered, well-drained corner of the garden, until conditions improve. The plants are set in a trench and the roots covered with soil.

a symmetrical arrangement of branches. Don't buy anything lopsided or tangled – both will cause problems later on.

Shrubs should generally have several stems, evenly spaced. Again, avoid damaged plants, or lopsided or untidy ones (unless that's the way the plant grows). If there's not an alternative plant, ask for a reduction in price. The manager will probably be only too keen for you to buy it.

Leaves Unless it's very late in the season, avoid any plant with yellowed or shrivelled leaves. The plant's been badly looked after, and may take a long time to recuperate. It is also worth checking the leaves for signs of unwelcome pests such as greenfly.

Flowers Don't worry if your plant isn't in flower – even if it's the right season. Some shrubs and most trees will need several more years' growth before they flower. Labelling can sometimes be inaccurate, so if the flowers turn out to be not what you expected – complain. Ask for the correct plant, or a refund (remember to keep the label).

Pots or bags? Plants grow equally well in either. Bags are much cheaper, and so should be the plant.

Weeds These are a useful indication of the plant's past, so have a look at them. If there are none, your plant has possibly been newly potted or bagged, and may deeply resent being replanted yet again. If the soil surface is tightly packed with dwarfed weeds, the plant will have been a year or two in its container. It will be root-bound and the soil will be exhausted. The roots will be difficult to disentangle when you're planting it. The ideal container plant should be sharing its container with a few healthy green weeds.

Soil preparation and planting

Your shrubs and trees will be the most permanent part of your planting, and are usually the most expensive to buy. If they are to do well, it is essential to supply the roots with the best conditions for growth.

Bare-rooted plants are all best planted in autumn, but if they don't arrive until early spring, don't worry. As long as they're not trying to open buds, they'll be all right. If your garden is on moderate to heavy soil, carry out as much advance soil preparation as you can in mid-autumn. By the time your plants arrive, the soil's nutrients, aeration, and drainage should be at their best. Leave preparing light, sandy soil until nearer the planting date.

Soil preparation for containerized plants is exactly similar, and is best carried out a month or two before planting. However, many garden centre plants are bought on impulse, so simply do as much as you can when actually planting.

Almost all soils are improved by the addition of rotted organic material, whether farm or stable manure, garden compost, spent hops or mushroom compost, or even peat mixed with bonemeal (a bucketful of the first to a handful of the second). Heavy soils need about a medium sized bucketful for each square metre (square yard). Light soils need 2–3 bucketfuls for each square metre (square yard).

Dig in the organic matter, at least two spits deep if possible, excavating the topsoil first, and forking half the organic material into the exposed, deeper layer, then adding the rest as you replace the topsoil. Planting holes should be at least 60 × 60cm (2 × 2ft) square, and should be 90 × 90cm (3 × 3ft) or more for all trees.

If you are planting in late autumn, bonemeal is a useful addition. Add about two good handfuls for each square metre (square yard), mixing it into the topsoil with a fork. Bonemeal contains plenty of slowly released phosphorus which will be needed by the developing roots.

When digging the area, large stones and weeds should be carefully removed; roots of bindweed, ground elder, couch grass, perennial thistle and horsetail are quite awful things to get amongst the roots of your plants. Most are easily sifted out of the soil as you dig.

If you have a limy or alkaline soil, and you want to grow rhododendrons, azaleas, some ericas and some camellias (some sorts of each of these are lime tolerant), it is possible to make pockets of acid soil by adding 3–4 bucketfuls of peat for each square metre (square yard). However, the desired effect of the peat eventually wears out, so you'll have to keep adding more. You might well find it simpler to grow them in big pots, or tubs. Better still, leave such plants for friends whose gardens have the right sort of soil, and concentrate on lime-tolerant plants: clematis, cotoneaster, buddleia, box, ceanothus, cistus, forsythia, fuchsia, laburnum, lilac (some with perfumes far more exciting than most azaleas, the best of all being the ancient Persian lilac), philadelphus, viburnum (with some wonderful winter-flowering sorts), and dozens of others.

Planting bare-rooted shrubs and trees
Though planting bare-rooted shrubs and trees is best done in late autumn when the soil is still relatively warm from the summer and the plants are not yet fully dormant, you may not always have that option. If your plants arrive in the depths of winter, have a look at your soil. If it's frozen or water-logged, wrap the plants' roots in damp sacking, straw, peat or compost. Do not let

them dry out. Don't store them in plastic sacks – rot easily sets in. Certainly don't drown them in a bucket of water. Store in a garage or shed until the soil is workable. Alternatively, if you're too busy to plant or store properly, plants can be heeled in, in a specially dug shallow trench in a sheltered part of the garden.

Remember that there is a quite major rule about planting: always make sure that the roots are spread out to their fullest extent. The planting hole must be large enough. Never plant a bush or tree with the roots all tangled up – the plants won't establish properly, won't ever anchor themselves well, and as the roots grow in thickness, they will begin to strangle each other.

Dig out a hole which is more than big enough. Make a shallow mound in the base and set the plant on the mound so that the roots spread naturally. If there are broken or damaged roots, trim them off with sharp secateurs. Crumble good topsoil, or a soil and compost mixture, in over the roots, shaking the plant gently during the process, so that the gaps between the roots fill pro-

perly. Firm the soil as you go, starting at the ends of the roots and working inwards.

Try to ensure that the planting level remains the same. On tree stems, it's usually easy to see the soil mark. If you can't, check to see if the plant is grafted (many trees are). If grafted you should be able to see a swollen oblique ring where the scion joins the stock and this should be left 5–7.5cm (2–3in) above ground level.

All trees (whether bare rooted or containerized), some large shrubs and all standard roses, will need the support of a stake. Hammer a suitable post into the bottom of the planting hole before you put the plant into position. This way, you'll avoid damaging the roots, as well as giving extra stability. The top of the post must reach only to just below the lowest branch. If it projects into the crown, nearby branches will get badly damaged in the first gale.

Planting containerized trees and shrubs
Always remove the plant from whatever container it's in – even whalehide pots. Have a look at the base of the root ball. If

1 *Planting holes for shrubs should be at least 60cm (2ft) square and plenty of organic matter, such as peat, worked into the lower soil.*
2 *With containerized shrubs, the top of the root ball should be slightly below soil level. Do not disturb the ball of roots when planting.*
3 *Return fine soil round the root ball, firming it with your heels as you proceed.*
4 *Finally, tidy up the surface of the soil to remove footprints.*

Left: *The eight shrubs are:* **1** *juniper (*Juniperus × media *'Pfitzerana Aurea'),* **2** *firethorn (*Pyracantha *'Orange Glow'),* **3** *lavender (*Lavandula angustifolia *'Munstead'),* **4** *veronica (*Hebe *'Autumn Glory'),* **5** *stag's-horn sumach (*Rhus typhina *'Laciniata'),* **6** *viburnum (*Viburnum × burkwoodii*),* **7** *broom (*Cytisus × kewensis*),* **8** *barberry (*Berberis thunbergii *'Atropurpurea'). One square = 1 metre.*

With careful choice of shrubs, even a small shrub border can be interesting and colourful throughout the four seasons. Here, only eight kinds of shrubs have been used, yet there is marvellous contrast in shape, colour and texture.

there's a thick coil of roots at the base, try to uncoil them as much as you can without doing major damage. When planting, spread out the uncoiled roots as if you were planting a bare-rooted plant. Try not to break up the rest of the root ball too much.

Once planted, water generously. Thereafter, check every day or so, especially in hot weather, and water at the least sign of drooping leaves.

Spacing and interplanting
When deciding where to plant, remember that the spacing of plants is very important. You will need to know the spread of a plant as well as its eventual height. These measurements are quite as important for shrubs as well as trees – climbers need

checking, too, for there's no point in planting, say, a *Clematis montana* against a bungalow wall, where it will be up over the roof and around the chimneys in a season.

Thinking ahead will pay dividends and, before settling on where to plant anything, it is also worth considering how new additions will fit in colour-wise. Bright colours can look wonderful but, as a general rule, simplicity is best: try to avoid setting dozens of different plants, each with a contrastingly bright colour, too closely together.

Getting a garden to look 'right' isn't difficult, but you do need to look at your trees and shrubs, examine how they grow, how they look with their neighbours, or work out how they are likely to look with any new additions you make.

Shrubs and trees are often planted too closely, for an instant effect. In a season or two, plants are cramped, growing and flowering far less well than they should, and becoming more prone to pests and diseases. Proper spacing means, sadly, an empty-looking garden for a year or two, but patience really does have its rewards.

It's always tempting to do something with the empty ground – planting annuals or herbaceous perennials. While this will give you a quick dash of colour, if you've prepared the soil properly, the vigorous vegetation will absorb all the nutrients that you've carefully dug in, as well as possibly shading out your chosen, long-term plants.

If you can possibly do so, avoid any inter-planting. If you must have colour, choose low-growing annuals (candytuft, French marigold, annual pinks, night-scented stock and antirrhinum are all useful). Tall-growing annuals, and most herbaceous plants, will soon swamp the chosen plants and make them grow even more slowly.

An alternative idea (more expensive, too), is to include in the shrub and tree planting some fast growing and showy sorts, to discard once the choicer ones need the space. Tree lupin, rock rose, and various sorts of broom are useful for this; lupin and broom improve the soil as well. However, it takes almost as much self-discipline to remove the 'flashy' shrubs when you ought to (they're usually at gorgeous maturity by then), as it does not to plant them in the first place.

If you're replacing a shrub, or want to insert one in an already mature border, make sure that not only do you prepare its site properly, but that you also clear enough surrounding vegetation to give it a chance to grow. Nothing is more frustrating than seeing a tiny twig get elderly but no bigger because your other plants won't let it grow. If possible, feed it with liquid manure once a fortnight for its first year.

Avoiding rose sickness

If your garden has got an old rose bed that you want to replant with yet more roses, beware. Your new plants may not flourish if they have been budded onto the same sort of rootstock that supported the ones you've thrown out. If at all possible, use a new site, or excavate the old one to a depth of 75cm–1m (30–36in) and replace with soil from another part of the garden. Remember to keep the top spit (one spade's depth) of soil separate when excavating, so that you can replace it on the top. Species roses, or roses grown on their own roots are often not affected by rose sickness so such preparations will not be necessary.

Aftercare

Once your newly purchased trees and shrubs are planted, certain routine aftercare procedures will help ensure that your plants get off to a good start.

Protection

Some plants, particularly evergreens and conifers, need a certain amount of help and protection from wind and hot sunshine when newly planted. If possible, set up some sort of screening from both. Either use a proper windbreak netting (always useful elsewhere in the garden, especially among vegetables and salad crops), or use split polythene sacks. Remember that it's a shelter, not a greenhouse, so don't enclose the plants too tightly.

Watering

Bare-rooted plants should begin new root formation in early spring, and soon become reasonably self-supporting. However, keep checking the leaves through late spring and summer, and water when necessary. Summer planted container plants of all sorts, but trees especially, take time to establish a root system beyond the original confines of the old container. If you don't pay them sufficient attention, they can collapse very quickly. They should, though, be self-supporting by their second summer.

Feeding

Unless your shrubs and trees find themselves in highly uncongenial situations, they'll grow. Except for the few that *need* poor soil, to get the very best out of your plants keep them well fed, particularly for the first couple of years. There's no point in feeding a bush 3m (10ft) across, or a tree that's as high as the house; although you will probably have to feed plants growing beside or beneath them.

Give plants an annual dressing of bone-meal in winter or early spring, or of chemical fertilizers in mid-spring. Much better, if you can manage it, is to give an annual mulch of compost or rotted manure – lightly forking it into the ground, as long as there are no nearby bulbs. In general, the plants' roots occupy an area more or less equal to the spread of the branches – so the plant itself gives you some idea of the most useful area to feed.

Deadheading

If you've all the time in the world, or a tiny garden, deadheading is worth doing for most of your plants. If you can't do it, don't worry, though it does help prolong the season of flowering of some varieties of rose. It does also help subsequent flowering in rhododendrons.

The planting scheme season by season

1.*Spring, with viburnum and broom in flower.*

2.*Summer, with flowers on firethorn, barberry, lavender and veronica.*

3.*Autumn, with berries on firethorn and barberry, and coloured foliage of stag's-horn sumach.*

4.*Winter, the juniper foliage comes into its own, and the firethorn is still in berry.*

CHAPTER 2

TRAINING AND PRUNING

To keep shrubs and trees within bounds, looking good and flowering well, some training and pruning may be necessary. It is not at all difficult if you understand the reasoning behind it.

In nature, shrubs and trees only get pruned in the most random way – by bad weather or grazing animals. In the garden, pruning is essential for quite a number of plants, to keep them within the space you can provide, to keep them flowering properly, or producing decorative foliage or stems. Pruning can also keep the plants well-shaped, though this depends rather on your 'eye' for such things.

Pruning also contributes to your plants' health by removing dead or dying branches. By avoiding the build up of dense tangles of twigs, it will also reduce the likelihood of fungal infection or insect attack.

Most new gardeners view the need to prune with some alarm. The actual act of pruning isn't at all difficult – the most important thing is to use a properly sharpened tool. Secateurs are the most useful, and as you'll need them for much of the year, buy the best ones that you can. Never use secateurs to cut through a branch that is too thick for them. Twisting the secateurs round in a tearing motion to complete the cut tears both wood and bark, and leaves a very untidy wound – a future site for infection. Make sure that the cutting blade remains sharp – it's not difficult to ensure.

For branches over 20mm (¾in) thick, use a pair of long-handled pruners (also useful for rose suckers). These have much more powerful cutting heads, and with the extra leverage of the handles, will cut nearly anything that you can get between the jaws.

Alternatively, use a pruning saw. Most of these have fine teeth on one edge and coarse ones on the other. Use the first set on hard woods, the other on soft. The main disadvantage of such saws is that the edge not in use can damage nearby branches. Some gardeners prefer saws with a curved and single-edge blade; these are much more useful when working in confined spaces.

The cleanest cut

Good secateurs or pruners give good cuts. If using a saw, try to support the end of the branch you're cutting, otherwise its weight will tear apart the wood below the cut. If there are torn and ragged parts, tidy them up with a sharp knife and the plant will soon heal itself.

If at all possible, small cuts should be slightly sloping from the horizontal. It's best to make large ones fairly vertical – that way, water won't collect on bare wood and start it rotting. Commercial wood wound sealers may be useful.

If buds are visible, cut just above an outwards facing one. This will ensure that new growth will be in a useful direction. If you cut too far above a bud, you'll eventually be left with a spur of dead wood, which will become unsightly, and an entry point for infection.

On thicker wood, buds can be difficult to see. You'll just have to cut where it's most convenient, and hope that there's a bud nearby. If several develop, remove the ones you don't want.

To prune or not to prune?

Few small shrubs (see Chapter 5) need anything beyond removing dead or diseased wood, and shaping, if branches grow in awkward directions or at awkward angles. Larger ones that need little work include Mexican orange blossom, *(Choisya ternata)*, *Corylopsis*, all the cotoneasters and daphnes, euonymus, genistas, witch hazels (though you'll be cutting sprigs to take indoors) hibiscus, some hydrangeas, most mahonias, olearias, skimmias, viburnums, and some of the gorgeous 'old' shrub roses.

There are five main groups of shrubs that do need pruning, plus climbers, each requiring a separate treatment. It's usually easy to decide which group your various shrubs fall into, and then you can prune them accordingly.

Early-flowering deciduous shrubs

In this group are some of the most popular and colourful sorts, including forsythia, the flowering currants *(Ribes)*, weigelas, deutzias and the closely related mock oranges *(Philadelphus)*, and the spring-flowering spiraeas. Climbers in this group include *Clematis montana* and *C. alpina* and winter-flowering jasmine (see page 15).

In all of these, the flowers are carried on shoots that grew in the previous summer.

Opposite *Dogwoods can be pruned almost down to ground level, leaving the bases of shoots with one or two buds.* **Below** *Shrubs grown for coloured stems, like the shrubby dogwoods* (Cornus), *can be pruned each year in early spring to encourage plenty of new shoots, which have the best colour.*

Top left *Hardy fuchsias are pruned virtually to ground level in early spring each year, just before they come into growth. They will produce flowers on the new shoots.*
Above left *Sometimes, coloured-leaved shrubs can produce odd shoots with green leaves, as with this spiraea. Such shoots should be cut out as soon as they are noticed.*
Above right *Mock orange (Philadelphus) is pruned immediately after flowering, by cutting out completely, or back to new shoots lower down, all stems which have carried flowers.*

You should wait until they have finished flowering before you prune, otherwise flower-bearing shoots will be cut off.

There's no need to prune young plants until they have filled their allotted space. Later, when they're the size you need, try to prune at least every two to three years, cutting out tangled branches, or ones that cross and rub against one another, and anything dead or diseased.

Prune immediately after flowering has finished, so that there's plenty of time for the plant to put on new growth to give you yet more flowers next spring.

Summer flowering deciduous shrubs
These include all the buddleias, the fuchsias, many hydrangeas, caryopteris, and the late-flowering spiraeas. All these flower on branches that have grown in the current season; pruning has to be done in early spring just before they start into growth. All should be pruned annually once they are big enough for your garden.

You can, if need be, cut the previous season's growth right back, either to ground level for some fuchsias, or to fairly short stumps, as in buddleias. It depends on how big you want the shrubs to be. Un-pruned buddleias can be vast, and dramatic looking, too. However, heavy pruning often improves their flowering.

The hortensia and lacecap hydrangeas

need rather less severe treatment, simply cutting off each faded flower head back to a healthy-looking bud, and removing any very weak growth at the same time is all that is necessary.

Shrubs grown for leaves or stems
These can be left unpruned if you like, but quite a number can be treated almost like herbaceous perennials, or cut back to ground level in early spring. The fast-growing shoots produced in the following summer are lush and large-leaved, and can make a dramatic contrast to your other plants.

The coloured stemmed dogwoods (*Cornus*), willows (*Salix*) and brambles (*Rubus*) are treated like this, as are the lovely smoke tree (*Cotinus coggygria*), the huge-leaved foxglove tree (*Paulownia*), some of the variegated sorts of the common elder (*Sambucus*), and some aralias. If you are a flower arranger, try using this technique on eucalyptus, and you'll get plenty of juvenile, round blue foliage ideal for cutting.

Evergreens
Early-flowering rhododendrons, azaleas, camellias, and the lovely, perfumed *Osmanthus* do not need pruning. If you need to cut them back do so immediately after flowering has finished. If you have the time to deadhead the rhododendrons, be careful of the young growth buds growing

at the base of the flower stalks.

How summer-flowering evergreens are pruned depends on the flowers. In most cases, clip the shrubs over once flowering has finished. For lavenders, use hedge shears. For hebes, just nip out old flower spikes, and do a little shaping.

If the flowers are unimportant, as in cotton lavender *(Santolina),* the senecios, and other grey-foliaged plants, prune them back in late spring. Shears will do for cotton lavenders, secateurs for the rest.

Foliage evergreens, such as laurel, the various splendid hollies, aucubas and elaeagnus, need as little pruning as possible consistent with a good shape. Variegated forms sometimes grow all-green shoots. Cut these out when they appear. Always use secateurs, not hedge trimmers or shears. For heathers, trimmers or shears are excellent. All need cutting back as soon as the flowers have faded.

Wall shrubs
This diverse group consists in general of slightly tender plants that are grown against walls to give them some shelter from cold and wind. Common examples include pyra-canthas, ceanothus, winter jasmine, and *Garrya elliptica.* There are, though, some splendid, less common plants, such as *Cytisus battandieri, Berberidopsis,* and others.

For most wall shrubs, initial pruning sets up the structure of the young plant. Later pruning takes out vigorous shoots growing away from the wall, and those not needed for tying in and training. Mature plants are pruned as for their free-standing counter-parts. Evergreen ceanothus are pruned immediately after flowering. The later flowering sorts (all deciduous) are pruned in early spring. Shorten any over-vigorous growth and remove weak shoots.

Climbers
Self-clinging climbers, such as, ivy, Virginia creeper, and climbing hydrangea, need no regular pruning. Growth liable to block gutters, or obscure the windows, can be removed at almost any time, though winter is best. Climbers always look best when luxuriant, so just keep them within bounds.

Twiners, such as clematis, honeysuckle, jasmine and wisteria need some care. Early-flowering clematis, such as *C. montana* and *C. alpina* are pruned, if need

Wisterias need regular pruning to prevent a tangled mass of growth. The new side shoots from the main framework of branches should be shortened in late summer and again in winter.

be, as soon as they have flowered. Summer flowering ones are often cut back to 75cm (30in) in late winter. Thin honeysuckles of all sorts after flowering. Wisterias have their long, whip-like shoots cut back to within 15cm (6in) of their base in late summer. The flower buds form along the spurs that remain. If possible, the spurs themselves are again pruned, in the depths of winter, to just ahead of flower buds, which are fatter-looking than leaf buds.

Renovation

If you've taken over an old garden, you may find some immense and tangled shrubs that don't actually add anything to the charms of your garden. If you don't feel like grubbing them out and starting again, it's usually possible to prune right back to a few basic branches, or even trunks. Do this in winter, sealing major wounds with a sealant. Don't worry if you can't see any buds – there will be plenty hidden in the bark. Mulch the plants with manure, or peat mixed with bonemeal.

Most deciduous shrubs will produce masses of new growth. With this you will have to be ruthless, allowing only a few new shoots from each old branch. Not all evergreens will respond to drastic cutting back and may even die. It's worth trying to take a few cuttings just in case this does happen (see Chapter 3).

Suckers

Some shrubs 'run' underground, producing new plants some distance away. The new ones are generally easily pulled up – they can make useful presents for gardening friends. The worst sort of suckers are produced by plants which have been grafted onto vigorous stock. Lilacs, roses and witch hazels are typical examples. As the sucker is produced by the rootstock, it won't look at all like the plant above. Worse, if allowed to grow, it will absorb nutrients that ought to be going to the plant you actually want. Young suckers are often difficult to see when the main plant is in leaf, so always have a careful look in autumn. If you find any, scrape the soil away from the base, then cut them out as far down as you can get. Pruners are often more use for this job than secateurs.

Pruning trees

Pruning mature trees is a job best left to professionals. It's an arduous and dangerous task for an amateur. However, if you've planted some young trees, there are several jobs you do need to do. Small-growing trees are often happy to turn themselves in to big bushes, so if you want

Wall-trained roses which have been neglected can be hard pruned in winter.
1 *This tangled mass of growth is in need of drastic thinning.*
2 *Start by cutting out any dead and diseased wood, and then remove the oldest.*
3 *Try to leave young stems, which will flower the following summer, and tie them in with soft garden string.*
4 *Space out the stems as evenly as possible.*

to keep them as standards, keep pruning off shoots that start to develop from the main stem. You might also find that the crown starts too low down so, as the crown starts to develop, you can remove the lower branches. Prune in midwinter.

Pruning hedges

The time to clip or trim a hedge depends on what type of hedge it is, especially whether it's evergreen or deciduous, whether it's supposed to flower (as in informal hedges), and whether it's newly planted or getting mature. Newly planted deciduous hedges are best cut back hard to within 23–30cm (9–12in) of ground level in early spring. Evergreens, such as privet or *Lonicera nitida* may be similarly pruned. Yew, holly, and the popular Lawson cypress are best not trimmed in any major way – just pinch out the tips of the more vigorous shoots. Beech and hornbeam should not be pruned at all for the first two years of growth.

Later, as the plants develop, encourage good, bushy growth by clipping the hedge into a wedge shape, wider at the base then at the top. Don't let the plants take over, otherwise you'll soon have a hedge full of growth at the top, with bare and leafless stems beneath.

Large-leaved evergreens like holly and laurel are better trimmed using secateurs, rather than shears or trimmers. Unfortunately, it's a time-consuming job, needing doing once or twice a year. However, a well-grown holly hedge looks quite marvellous, and worth all the trouble. Shears or trimmers damage more leaves than they cut, resulting in a messy finish.

Allow hedges to nearly reach the height you want, before you 'stop' them by cutting out the leaders. Overgrown hedges of blackthorn, hornbeam, and thorn can usually be rejuvenated by hard cutting during the winter months. Yew, box, laurel and privet can all be drastically cut back, preferably in early spring, when the new growth that the cutting stimulates won't be hurt by frost. You'll have to get used to the mutilated trunks for a year or two, but after that, you'll have a nice, fresh hedge.

Topiary

Really a specialized sort of hedging, topiary has been in and out of fashion since at least Roman times. The Romans tried most of the possibilities too, carving out of their box bushes, full-scale hunts and heraldic animals, as well as more formal pyramids, obelisks and urns. 'Topiarius' was the Roman word for gardener.

Nowadays, formal topiary is mostly found in grand gardens that can carry the heavy expense of endless clipping, but other sorts of topiary can look lovely in small gardens – especially of country cottages – and it can be great fun to experiment.

Simplest of all, and often visually the most effective, are globes, cubes and, perhaps, obelisks. These look good making ends or entrances in hedges, or for making the corners or centres of formal beds (an obelisk of yew, surrounded by ferns, low annuals, or even bush roses, can look very attractive).

Peacocks, chess pieces, or tiered 'cake stands' need to be on a large scale to be effective, and small gardens can only usually support one or two. If you've got the right sort of house, the traditional place to put them is in the front garden, especially beside the gate.

However, topiary can form almost any shape you like, from sentry boxes (the most splendid ones large enough to hold seats and a table), elephants, whole sitting-rooms, four-poster beds or battleships.

Holly isn't actually very much use as a

Below *Shears can be used to trim small-leaved hedging plants; larger-leaved kinds are best pruned with a pair of secateurs.*

Bottom *Examples of formal hedges (from left to right):*
Chinese honeysuckle
Common yew
Common holly
Laurel
Hornbeam
Common beech
Golden privet
Leyland cypress

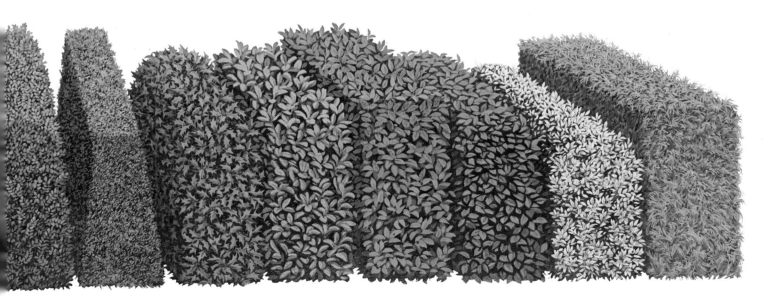

Above *Animals of various kinds are favourite subjects for topiary, a specialized sort of hedging which has been in and out of fashion at least since Roman times.*
Above right *Today, formal topiary is mostly found in grand gardens, a notable example being this 'chess set' at Haseley Court in Oxfordshire.*

topiary plant, though yew and box are excellent. *Lonicera nitida* and privet are rather less good.

Topiary is fairly easily made. Some complex examples are made up along a wirework frame, the young branches trained as they grow. These form the 'bones', the eventual side branches forming the 'flesh'. Start topiary from young plants, it isn't generally possible to cut down an old bush and turn it into a satisfactory piece.

Quick topiary

Real topiary takes time, patience and energy. It is possible to make quite acceptable garden features, using simple shapes and quick-growing climbers. One of the best ways is to make up the shape you want, using wire netting on some sort of rigid frame – bamboo poles for obelisks. Then train up several plants of a climber, pinching out as regularly as you can, until the netting is covered. The most effective covering is of ivy, using perhaps one of the decorative forms (*Hedera helix* 'Caenwoodiana' is excellent).

If you're really in a hurry, and have an ivy plant somewhere that you can raid for cuttings, pack the wire frame with damp moss, and push in ivy cuttings over the whole surface. Keep damp – a spray is a good device to use for watering. Soon, the ivy should root into the moss, and eventally into the ground. Clip annually in winter.

Care

If you decide to go for the grandest sort of topiary, and plant young yew bushes, make sure that the soil is fertile and well drained. Allow new plants a year before starting to shape them. Prune in early winter, and in the following summer, pinch back side shoots to encourage bushy growth. Keep

the plants growing fast by mulching with compost or lawn clippings, and keep well watered in dry weather.

Topiary in pots

A pleasant fashion is returning to favour, and it's now possible to buy standard bay trees with a ball-shaped crown, as well as obelisks and spheres of box. They're quite expensive to buy, but perfectly easy to grow at home. If you want to make some, remember that the pots need fairly constant attention, but also that you can use a much wider range of species. Making 'standard' plants is described below, but to make simple, low-growing shapes, try using cotton lavender for silvery ones, gold-variegated box, and most of the shrubby herbs (hyssop is especially good).

Formal training

While many gardeners like their gardens to look as natural as possible, a little formality can make an exciting contrast. Formal hedges, of course, are entirely artificial, and so is topiary, but shrubs, trees and climbers can be used in other formal ways. 'Standard' bushes, whether in the open ground or in pots, can look splendid. Tunnels, pergolas and arches are all lovely garden features which require a little skill in training, and even straightforward wall shrubs will need a little work.

Standard trained plants looks especially good in patios or courtyards, by doorways or entrances. Standard roses look wonderful by paths or in formal gardens. Roses are the most difficult to make (see Chapter 3), but the others are easy, especially if you can start with a young, single stemmed, plant – perhaps a cutting you've rooted.

Even if they're intended for the open ground, it's usually best to start them off in

a 9cm (3½in) pot. Add a pea cane for support, tying the young stem to the cane at 5cm (2in) intervals; the sort of wire ties used for freezer bags are useful for this. Feed regularly, and rub off any buds that develop from the main stem. The idea is to get maximum growth from the only growth point, and a nice, straight stem. Re-pot, regularly, as soon as the roots have filled the available soil. If the plants try to flower (and if you let them get pot bound, they certainly will), don't be greedy; remove all flower buds straight away.

As you re-pot, remove the old cane, and

Climbing roses trained over arches or pergolas make lovely garden features and require very little skill in pruning and training.

substitute a taller one. Once the main stem is tall enough, let the leading shoot produce four pairs of (or four single) leaves beyond the top of the support, then pinch out the growing point. When new shoots form from the top four growing points – or nodes – pinch out their growing tips when they're 10cm (4in) long. Pinch out subsequent shoots that grow from those when they are also 10cm (4in) long.

If you're using a flowering plant, perhaps a fuchsia, a lantana, a geranium, or even an orange or a grapefruit seedling, or most grandly of all, a wisteria, allow it to flower. If you're training a foliage plant, such as bay, box or laurel, or something tender – like one of the *Helichrysum* species – you'll need to keep pinching out the growing shoots.

Supporting plants

Many wall shrubs and a number of climbers need some sort of support. Most look best when grown informally, though some make handsome espaliers or fans (these two sorts of training are essential for most major fruit, but can also look excellent using pyracanthas or cotoneasters).

Excellent wall shrubs that don't need support include various sorts of ceanothus, *Garrya elliptica*, pyracantha and the less tough sorts of escallonia.

For those that need support (and that includes all the 'climbing' and 'rambler' roses) as well as the twining sorts of climber, you'll need to set up some sort of framework. This can consist of an arrangement of wires stretched through vine eyes, or trellis work or even wire netting attached to the wall.

A system of wires is generally the best support in the long run. Although you'll have to tie in the soft stems of plants that won't support themselves, it's easy to untie them in the future, should you need to carry out pruning, or to paint or point the wall behind. It's important to remember that large climbers can weigh a great deal, so ensure that the wires are anchored properly, and can be tightened if they stretch.

Trellis work can look very pretty on suitable houses, and can look particularly nice if it's of unpainted wood. White plastic, while long lasting, can sometimes look so bright and shiny that no plant can compete. Once a plant, particularly a vigorous climber like *Clematis montana* or jasmine, has become thoroughly attached to the trellis, it can be impossible to detach it. This is especially annoying if you need to prune.

Wire netting is cheap and easily attached, and it's easy to thread through the stems as they grow. However, it makes any subsequent thinning virtually impossible. If you eventually want to remove the plant, the netting

has to come off, too. Roses are particularly bad, for you are then left with an unmanageable sheet of fiercely armoured vegetation, reinforced with steel mesh.

Pergolas and arches

Pergolas and arches can be constructed of anything from unbarked poles (nice in cottage gardens), to grand affairs of stone columns and dressed wood. As with wall plants, remember that the weight of vegetation can become quite large, and that gales can be a major problem – build the supports as securely as you can.

When planting them up, include a few foliage climbers, such as *Vitis vinifera* 'Brandt' or the purple leafed vines, or the Dutchman's Pipe *(Aristolochia)*. This will ensure that even when nothing is in flower, the overall appearance will still be attractive. It's always tempting to add something fast growing, like a Russian vine or a rampant clematis. If you do want to use these plants, it's best to give them a structure all to themselves (they're quite nice enough), or they'll quickly swamp slower-growing subjects. The Russian vine in particular, is an excellent choice for covering unwanted sheds and the like.

In the early stages of growth, tie in young shoots. It's often neater to tie them to suitable placed nails, rather than tie them directly to part of the structure.

Laburnum, hornbeam or fruit tunnels look wonderful when mature, but are expensive things to build and maintain. The basic structure needs to be of metal, with regularly spaced wires stretched between them. Apples are espaliered along the wires, but laburnum stems, being pliable, can be threaded in between them.

Tripods

If you have a new and empty garden, tripods planted with climbers can be a useful means of getting some fast bulk and height. In their simplest form, they can be built with three 3m (10ft) poles (unbarked if possible), sunk 45cm (18in) into the ground, and tied at the top to make a rough wigwam. Carry the string on down between the poles to make a framework to help the climbers get a hold. Tripods like these will support rambler roses, or plant them up with clematis (especially ones that are easily propagated – most often the early-flowering species), or anything else you like. Honeysuckles are good.

They can either be left as a permanent feature of the garden, or can be removed when the permanent shrubs in the garden have grown sufficiently to give you enough visual height. It's worth taking cuttings, if you dismantle a tripod.

CHAPTER 3

MAKING MORE

Propagating your own shrubs and trees is pleasurable as well as economic. It is an easy way to fill out a new garden, or change the look of an old one, virtually for free. Any extra plants can be shared among friends or neighbours, so you can never have too many.

Some shrubs and trees can be propagated as easily as herbaceous plants – by division. Many have underground stems which grow through the soil, producing roots as they go, then turning upwards into the light to make a new plant. Some plants produce underground stems so energetically that they become almost a nuisance – in which case the new plants are called 'suckers'. However, if you have a new garden, such plants are remarkably useful, for you'll soon have plenty of material – and the garden will rapidly appear mature. Examples of suckering shrubs are all the japonicas *(Chaenomeles)*, some of the low-growing hypericums and artemisias, the pernettyas, the decorative sorts of raspberry and blackberry *(Rubus)*, the exotic, perfumed clerodendrons, and the equally exotic but more commonly planted sumach *(Rhus typhina)*, as well as lilacs and roses.

Lilacs and roses are often grafted, so the suckers are part of the rootstock, and aren't worth keeping. However, if you've found lilacs or roses that have been propagated from cuttings – and so are on their own roots – then the suckers will be the same as the flowering part of the plant and are worth keeping.

The best time to remove suckers for propagation purposes is in autumn or early spring. There often isn't all that much in the way of root, so cut the leafy part back to about 10cm (4in).

Other shrubs and trees produce what are in effect suckers, but with almost non-existent underground 'stolons', so that the centre of the plant becomes a mass of upright stems, each one with some roots of its own. These can often be separated from the main plant, either by digging the whole thing up and hacking them apart with a spade, or by forcing a trowel down into the clump and levering a few of the outer stems away from the centre.

Again, this is best done in autumn or early spring, cutting the shoot back so that the young roots will be able to support it. Plants that can be treated like this include hazels *(Corylus)*, fuchsias, some mock oranges *(Philadelphus)*, amelanchiers, winter-flowering viburnums, the eating quince *(Cydonia)*, some mahonias, most barberries *(Berberis)*, kerrias and spiraeas, The snowberries *(Symphoricarpos)*, will produce so many shoots as to positively menace your garden.

Layering

Division is easy because at no time is your young plant without roots in the way that a cutting is. However, there's a very useful garden technique intermediate between division and taking cuttings: layering.

The basic sort of layering is useful for most climbers, and shrubs with branches near enough the ground, or flexible enough, to peg them to the soil. For most suitable plants, start the job in mid-spring, choosing a healthy shoot that grew last year. Using a sharp knife, make a longish cut on the underside, if possible slicing along beneath the point from which a leaf grows.

Carefully bend the whole stem to the ground (take care that it doesn't snap at the cut – or you'll have a cutting), and peg the cut shoot to the ground – or even just weight it down with a stone. The cut must be in contact with the soil, or even slightly buried. Some gardeners like to keep the cut open, using a matchstick as a wedge. The cut should be several centimetres (inches) from the branch's tip – up to 45cm (18in) from it. You'll get a better shaped young plant if you can tie the free length to a short, upright cane, though this needs great care if you aren't to snap the stem.

The layers should have rooted by late autumn. To check that rooting has taken place, give a gentle tug. If it has, simply cut the young plant away from the parent, and replant elsewhere.

Good plants for layering include all rambling and climbing roses, many rhododendrons, viburnums, magnolias, laurels, aucubas and other evergreens. Layering is an especially good way to propagate wisterias. Start layering clematis in autumn, using one-year-old or two-year-old stems. Climbing honeysuckles are also best started off in the autumn.

Long stems can be layered in several

Opposite One of the easiest and most successful ways of propagating a wide range of shrubs, including viburnum shown here, is by layering young stems in spring. The stems root where they are pegged down into the soil. Some will be rooted by the autumn of the same year, while other plants take at least a year to form a root system.

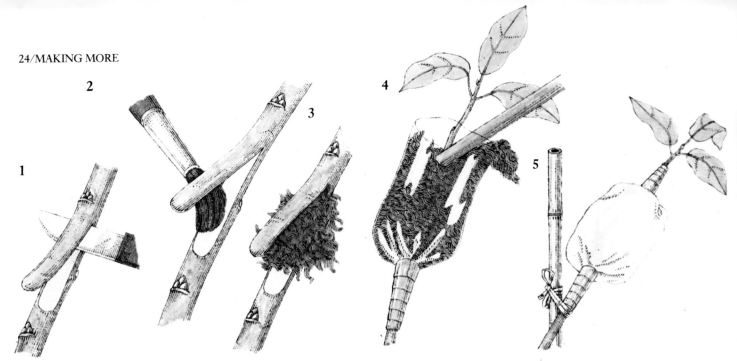

Air layering is an easy way of propagating trees and shrubs, particularly camellias, cherry and plum, and rhododendrons.
1 Prepare a young stem by cutting a tongue about 5cm (2in) long.
2 Dust the cut surfaces with a hormone rooting powder to encourage rooting.
3 Keep the tongue open by packing it with moist sphagnum moss.
4 A polythene sleeve is partially secured to the stem, and then filled with moist sphagnum moss, into which the stem will root.
5 Finally, the sleeve is completely sealed, using waterproof tape.

places, a process called serpentine layering. Honeysuckle will root at every node if you weight it down along the length of the stem.

Stooling
Of course, not all your shrubs will have branches flexible enough to make them suitable for layering. Some of these, such as dogwood *(Cornus)* and ceanothus, can be stooled. Pile soil into the centre of the bush you want to propagate so that the bases of the branches are covered. During the course of the summer, these put out roots. In autumn and early winter, the piled-up soil is carefully removed and the rooted shoots detached.

There are various refinements, but most of them are of more interest to commercial nurseries. Stooling is particularly good for heathers *(Erica)* once they've grown leggy and you need some young plants.

Air layering
This is another easy method, especially useful if the tree or shrub has no low-level branches. There is none of the risk involved in taking cuttings, and you don't need a frame or propagator.

Air layering is similar to ordinary layering, except that the soil is replaced with damp moss and, to stop the moss drying out, it is wrapped in polythene. When air layering older plants, cut a tongue in the bark but do not sever the stem. Lift up the tongue of bark to leave the wood exposed. That way, the stem above your hoped-for layer won't break off if there's a gale. A handful of damp moss is wrapped around the sliced area, which is then wrapped in polythene. Tie off each end to make a sort of sausage. Use black polythene if you can – a cut-up rubbish bag is ideal. Though clear polythene does let you see when roots begin to form, it also lets weeds and algae grow.

Try to use healthy young shoots, about the thickness of a pencil, and of last summer's growth – do not use old and hard wood. Not all plants will layer in this way, but it is especially useful for camellias, various sorts of cherry and plum, and, most importantly, rhododendrons.

There are two disadvantages, though. Black polythene parcels look fairly awful, clustering in your bushes. Secondly, the young plants have very fragile roots, and need to be potted up with the very greatest care to avoid damaging them.

Cuttings
Taking cuttings of shrubs and trees is often easy, always good fun, and surprisingly productive. While some species can be tricky, hundreds upon hundreds of sorts will root easily. Sometimes you will need to know the right time of year to do it, and perhaps even a few 'tricks of the trade', but you will find that lots of your plants will grow from almost any twig stuck in the ground.

The most common cutting is taken from the top 10–15cm (4–6in) of stem, usually of what is called 'semi-mature' growth, with bark that is begining to turn brown. Carefully remove the lower leaves before inserting it in the soil.

A cutting made from the same sort of shoot, but still soft and sappy, is a 'soft' cutting, while fully ripe wood is called a 'hardwood' cutting. Cuttings can be made of sections of stem of almost any age, and even of single leaves with a fragment of stem attached (as in camellias, figs and vines for instance).

The simplest shrubs to take cuttings from are those which can tolerate fairly dry conditions. Sage, lavender, rosemary, rock rose *(Helianthemum)*, cistus, hebe, santolina and even hydrangea are suitable subjects. Take cuttings in summer, and insert them to about half their length in a pot of moist, sandy soil or soil-based seed compost. The latter is much better for the beginner than any of the peat-based composts. If you don't want to fuss with watering the pots, just plant the cuttings in a cool, shady part of the garden. Give the cuttings a light daily spray with water to keep them from wilting. Don't use the watering-can for this, or you will saturate the soil and the stems will rot.

For less tough shrubs and trees, including fuchsias, spiraeas, mock oranges *(Phila-delphus),* caryopteris, shrubby verbenas and most ceanothus, it's easy to stop the cuttings drying out by inserting them in a pot, then tying a clear polythene bag over the top. Stop the bag collapsing by using a few wire hoops to form a framework over the cuttings.

As conditions inside the bag will be extremely humid, it is worth spraying your cuttings with a general garden fungicide – though don't use too much, for some fungicides actually inhibit root formation as well as disease.

Early autumn is also an excellent time to take yet more cuttings, of trees as well as shrubs, hedging plants, and especially of roses. Many will 'do' in the open ground, and that's certainly the simplest way of starting up new hedges or edging. Remove the lower leaves and insert sprigs of privet, *Lonicera nitida,* box, holly, deutzia, or lavender, every 15–30cm (6–12in) along the centre line of where you want the hedge. Firm the soil around each cutting, then leave well alone.

A shady part of the garden can be used to root rambler, climbing and shrub roses – just line the cuttings out as if you were planting a hedge. You will find that some really need two seasons in the row before they're sufficiently established to move.

For slightly trickier material, it's worth having a cold frame. The still air inside it stops the unrooted material drying out, and the slightly less cold soil stops the cuttings going completely dormant. It's worth taking cuttings of whatever you need. You will certainly have some failures, but plenty of successes, too.

Conifers, such as cypresses, junipers, cedars and larches, will all root from 'heel' cuttings. These are small side branches pulled off larger ones, with a small strip of older wood at their bases. Some conifers ooze resin over the tear. The resin hardens and can prevent rooting, so try dipping the ends of spruce and fir cuttings in hot water for a few moments to stop this happening.

Propagation aids
Most garden centres sell powders or liquids containing the plant hormones essential for root formation. However, not all plants are interested in hormones from the outside world, and others need very particular concentrations – so the effects of using them, even under ideal circumstances, are variable.

However, the formulae usually also contain a fungicide, so even if the hormones don't help, the fungicide might result in more cuttings surviving to form roots.

Buy a new container annually, for the hormones gradually lose effectiveness. All things considered, they are worth using – but don't expect magically improved results. The thing that will drastically improve your results is gardening experience – so do not give up if your first few cuttings fail.

Many sorts of propagator are marketed, but only the largest ones are really useful. Small ones are difficult to keep at even temperatures – and anything that you can get to root in them you can probably root in the garden under a jam jar just as easily. A good quality cold frame, a soil-warming cable, and a good quality hand-spray will give you much better results.

Mist propagation is much talked about and there are even small kits available for the amateur gardener. The kits provide a

1

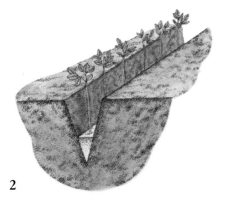

2

Many kinds of roses can be rooted from well-ripened cuttings in early autumn.
1 *Cuttings should be approximately 25cm (9in) in length, with the soft tip removed.*
2 *Set them out to about two-thirds of their depth in a slit trench lined with sharp sand for good drainage.*
It is important to choose a sheltered, shady part of the garden for rooting rose cuttings.

closed environment with a high degree of humidity control, and can provide short bursts of mist every few minutes. There are lots of problems with it, so unless you really want to propagate in a big way, don't bother with this method.

Being able to supply bottom heat to your cuttings is quite useful for anyone with a moderately large garden – and it is easily achieved by putting a soil-warming cable into one of your frames. It's as useful for raising seeds as it is for rooting some of the more difficult cuttings.

Seeds

All trees and shrubs produce seeds, so seeds seem initially a perfect way of getting new plants. However, many garden plants are, in fact, special, named varieties (a variety is a small sub-unit of a proper species), or hybrids (resulting from cross-breeding), and very few of them will come true from seed. Seedlings are sometimes quite different from the parent plant. The new plants might be more beautiful – or less. Indeed, that's one of the excitements of growing from seed.

Unfortunately, it's an excitement that is available to rather few gardeners, because growing large numbers of young plants, and waiting to see which are worth keeping, needs considerable space and time. Even so, seeds are a useful means of increasing shrubs that are not named varieties, or that will not increase easily from cuttings, such as daphnes. Hedging plants such as yew and hawthorn, are also suitable.

Almost without exception, all tree and shrub seeds should be sown in autumn, preferably in pots, and left outside all winter. The seed needs to be frozen, sometimes frozen and thawed several times, before it will consent to germinate. This process can be carried out in the fridge, but you will find that the natural process is generally more effective.

If the seed is very small, to stop it being splashed out of the soil, cover the pot or pan with a sheet of glass. You can stretch polythene over, but make sure that it's tightly done, or rain water will soon weigh the sheeting down onto the soil. Some seed, roses in particular, may need two full winters to break their dormancy. So, if nothing comes up the first spring, not all is lost.

If seeds you have ordered arrive late, then you will have to use your refrigerator. There's no special virtue in using the freezer compartment – the open shelves will do. If someone in the household objects to having pots of earth in the refrigerator, wrap the seeds in damp blotting paper or a coffee filter, put in a freezer bag, then chill. Dry seeds are often impervious to cold.

Budding and grafting

These techniques are scarcely used by amateurs, though budding is both easy and useful. It's by far the easiest way of increasing the hybrid sorts of rose (cuttings of these can be difficult to root). It is also useful if you want to increase tree fruits, or to make family trees, which have several varieties of a fruit growing from a single trunk. It's also useful if you want to make your own standard roses, standard or weeping trees, or even standard wisterias.

Budding is almost risk free. It uses only a few buds of the 'scion' (the plant you are wanting for its flowers or fruit), and hardly damages the 'stock' (the plant that provides the roots and the lowest part of the stem).

Once you have decided which plant you want to increase, you will have to get a supply of one or more stock plants. For roses, some lilacs and fruit trees, this can be easy. When suckers appear, simply dig them up carefully so that they have a few roots still attached, then replant elsewhere. Most stocks are of plants that reproduce easily – often from cuttings. Should you need a quantity, take cuttings in mid-summer, or in early autumn, to see which of them do best.

Budding works best during the summer. Unless you have both stock and scion potted up in a greenhouse, wait for moist, showery weather when the plants will be well filled with water. Avoid hot, dry days, if at all possible, or the buds you insert may dry out and die.

Look for plump buds in an 'axil' (the joint between stem and leaf stalk) on the current year's growth, and carefully cut it out using a very sharp knife. Special budding knives are available, though a sharp stainless steel kitchen parer will do. Start

Hybrid roses are best propagated by budding the varieties onto rootstocks during the summer.
1 A dormant bud, situated in a leaf axil, is removed as a shield-shaped piece of bark with a sliver of wood behind it. This sliver may be carefully removed.
2 At the bottom of the rootstock make a T-shaped cut in the bark and lift the two flaps.
3 Slide the bud down underneath the bark and trim off the top of the shield if it projects above the T-cut.
4 Bind in tightly with raffia or insulating tape, but leave the actual bud exposed.

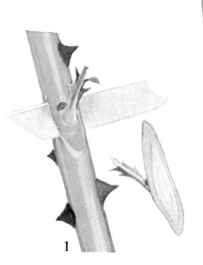

1

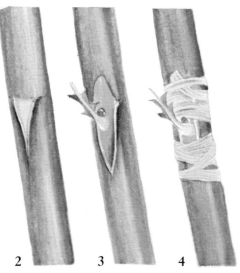

2   3   4

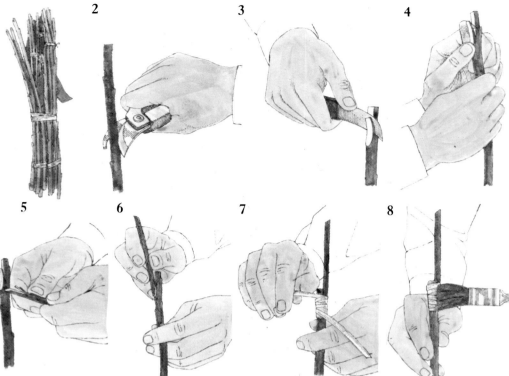

1   **2**   **3**   **4**

5   **6**   **7**   **8**

If you are feeling adventurous, you could try propagating trees by whip and tongue grafting, including fruit trees. As with budding, the variety to be propagated is put on to a suitable rootstock. Whip and tongue grafting is carried out in late winter/early spring.
1 Scions of the variety can be gathered in winter, bundled up and heeled in a spare piece of ground.
2 Scions should be prepared to about three or four buds in length.
3 The rootstock is prepared by first cutting off the top; a 2in (5cm) long rut is then made at the top, followed by a short downward cut to form a tongue.
4 The tongue must be of even thickness but not too thick.
5 Matching cuts are then made at the base of the scion.
6 The scion is fixed to the stock, with the tongues interlocking.
7 The union should be tightly bound with raffia or grafting tape.
8 It is then sealed with a suitable product such as tree-pruning paint.

the cut 20–25mm (¾–1in) above the bud, and gently curve it down to about the same distance below. The bud, complete with the oval sliver of wood beneath it, can then be lifted off. Trim away the leaf, but leave enough of its stalk to act as a handle for transporting the bud.

Some gardeners leave the oval of wood in position, but it's sometimes better to gently lever it away from the green bark. Go carefully, otherwise it may pull the all-important centre of the bud away as well, and you will have to start again. If the wood is unwilling to come away leave it in position.

Next, make a T-shaped incision into the bark of the stock, with the upright of the T running down its stem. Cut through the bark, but as little as possible into the wood below. Gently lever the bark away – budding knives are specially adapted to doing this, but a potato peeler will start you off quite well at the angles of the T. Enough has to be levered back to enable the bud and its shield to be slipped right down underneath the stock's bark.

Once the shield is in position – the inside of the base of the bud *must* be in contact with the wood of the stock – trim off the little handle and firmly bind the base and top of the T with insulating tape (easy to peel away afterwards), leaving the scion bud exposed. If there's too much of the top of the shield projecting above the T, trim it off with a very sharp blade.

In about three weeks the bud should have 'taken', in which case it will still be a nice

fresh green. If it hasn't, it will have gone brown. If all's well, leave the tape in position, but as soon as the bud begins to sprout, cut back the stock to just above the new bud.

How high up the stem of the stock you carry out budding depends on what you want. For bush roses, most bushes and trees, work as near ground level as you can. For standard roses, or weeping decorative trees, insert the bud where you want the clear stem to branch out. The stock may attempt to produce its own branches and these must be rubbed off.

If the bud fails, remove the tape, the failed bud, then retape. The wound should soon heal. It's possible to try several buds on the stock – as an insurance. If several 'take', prune to the lowest, or the stock will keep trying to take over.

Whip and tongue grafting, an alternative but equally effective way to increase trees and shrubs, is illustrated above.

Below *Grape vines can be propagated from eye cuttings. A portion of young stem, complete with bud, is taken in winter. The bark on the opposite side to the bud can be removed to encourage rooting. Press the cutting down into sandy compost and place in heat to encourage rooting.*

CHAPTER 4

PLANT PROBLEMS

Fortunately, ornamental trees and shrubs are much less vulnerable to pests and diseases than fruit, vegetables and herbaceous plants. Still, problems do occur from time to time, and it pays to be prepared, so you can solve them as quickly, effectively and economically as possible.

Pests come in many forms:
1 Cutworms and leatherjackets chew the roots of many plants.
2 Birds are notorious for stripping berries and damaging buds.
3 Caterpillars of various moths and butterflies eat holes in leaves.
4 Leaf miners are grubs which tunnel inside leaves.
5 Slugs and snails will eat almost any soft young growth.

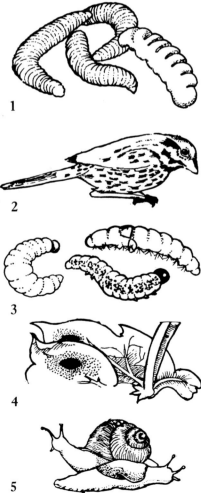

There are innumerable things that can go wrong with your garden plants, but very few things that actually do. The most important single thing that you can do, right from the very beginning, is to garden with your garden, not against it. Check the soil – dozens of sorts of soil test kits are available from garden centres and shops, most of which are inexpensive and easy to use – and take any corrective measures that are necessary, preferably before planting.

If your soil is especially acid, grow suitable, acid-loving plants, such as rhododendrons and heathers. If your garden has acid inner-city soil, the acidity probably isn't natural and can be corrected by adding lime and well-rotted manure or compost.

If your garden is on limestone, chalk or shell sand, it will be dry and alkaline. Again, you have a vast range of lime-loving plants from which to choose, and you will be able to create a lovely garden using the right plants. Some may very occasionally suffer from nutrient deficiencies, but this can be corrected by digging in plenty of organic matter and by feeding, as above. Sometimes iron and magnesium are held in by the alkaline soil itself and so are not available to your plants. (The main symptom is that the leaves will look yellow when they shouldn't). Either add peat, or buy 'sequestered' nutrient compounds (ones which the soil can't catch) and water these in.

On light soils, or in dry areas, drought can be a problem. Simplest is to plant only drought-resistant plants. If you have to keep watering endlessly, not only will you waste time you could probably spend doing something else, you'll probably also be washing precious nutrients out of the soil, and making even more work for yourself.

If your garden is wet or boggy, it is very much cheaper to buy plants that grow well with damp root conditions than it is to drain it.

However, by far the majority of gardens have fairly neutral soil, are reasonably well drained, and in reasonable 'heart'. With good basic maintenance, most garden plants should grow for you.

Chemical fertilizers

Apply all these with care, following the manufacturers' instructions to the letter. Oversupply of nutrients can damage plants' roots, or even alter the overall balance of other elements in the soil, causing problems.

If things do go wrong, there's most often a simple reason, and it's usually better to suspect disease, insect attack, seasonal factors, or a gardening 'mistake' than a deficiency in the soil.

However, if no plants will grow properly, there may be something radically wrong with your soil. It's possible to get your local agricultural college or horticultural advisory service to help (they'll charge a small fee), with a full soil analysis.

Garden pests

How much damage any pests do will vary from year to year. Almost every garden pest has its own enemies, and the balance between a pest and its predators changes. Remember that most pesticides also kill beneficial insect predators, and once the predators have gone, there's nothing to stop a subsequent build up (and triumph) of the pest. So, if possible, trap slugs and snails, then kill them by sprinkling salt over them. Rub greenfly off leaves and buds with your thumb and forefinger, or cut off infected shoots and burn them. Most importantly, make sure that your plants are growing well so that both you and they can tolerate slight amounts of damage.

Insecticides should really be a last resort for most insect pests, though they're a first resort for whitefly, scale insects and mealy bugs. These foreigners have no native predators, all are most common under glass.

Types of insecticide

These are now almost as various as the insects themselves. When choosing, check first that they will kill the pest you want to eradicate, then check that they won't damage the plant you want to save. If there are several that will do the job, check how long lasting they are. Persistent insecticides now available can remain lethal for up to two weeks, which will protect your plants, but will kill all sorts of other insects as well as the pest you want to control. If you need such a chemical, good ones to use are HCH and fenitrothion. Non-persistent sorts, such as derris, pyrethrum or resmethrin are lethal only for one day.

Many garden insecticides are contact poisons. Droplets of spray have to actually touch the pest concerned to be effective, hence the need for a good sprayer, and a good, thorough soaking of the plant, including the leaf undersides.

Systemic insecticides are actually absorbed by the plant, and any insect eating it, or sucking its juices, is poisoned. The chemicals are circulated throughout the plant, so insects feeding some distance from the parts you've actually sprayed are also killed. Systemic insecticides are consequently useful for plants with dense foliage which is difficult to spray.

If using a contact spray, try to avoid spraying open flowers, and try to spray in the evening. That way, you will avoid killing bees and butterflies. If using a systemic insecticide, remember that you will be killing anything that visits the flowers.

Spray left over in the sprayer needs treating with care, so try not to make up more than you need for the immediate job. Most sprays are lethal to aquatic life, so don't let them get into ponds, streams, or even the sewage system. Many are also poisonous to mammals, so don't let the spray drift onto you, your children or your pets.

What to look out for

Aphids, including greenfly, blackfly and the reddish, rose aphids, but not whitefly, do not move around much, so they're often easily seen. Other mobile pests often feed at night, so most gardeners don't see them. Visible symptoms of such pests are curled-up leaves (caused by aphids or caterpillars), a peppering of tiny holes in the leaves (caused by capsids or earwigs), rusty-looking leaves, sometimes with a covering of fine webbing (caused by red spider), oblong sections chewed from the leaf margins (caused by weevils), rounded sections removed from the margins of rose leaves (caused by the leaf-cutting bee) and leaves with pale tracks excavated between upper and lower surface (caused by leaf miners, especially in holly). Lastly, disappearing fruits or berries are caused by various birds and small mammals.

Diseases

Plant diseases are caused by fungi, bacteria or viruses. Though bacterial and viral diseases are of great importance in the kitchen garden, they are hardly ever problems in the ornamental garden – and then mostly affect herbaceous plants.

Fungal diseases are slightly more of a problem. These are more commonly found in ornamental forms of kitchen garden plants, such as flowering almonds, plums and apricots, or in some of the highly bred shrubs and climbers, especially some roses and clematis. In general, the closer a plant is to its wild form, the less prone it is to attack, and the more capable it is of withstanding one.

Many sorts of fungal infection get to work inside the plant's tissues, so by the time you see the effects, the disease may be difficult to cure. Many fungi, such as peach leaf curl and rose blackspot, overwinter in fallen fruit, leaves or twigs, so garden hygiene can play an important role in preventing infection. Some fungi have spores so light that they're virtually always present in the atmosphere, so there's nothing you can do to keep them out of your garden. However, the spores can't penetrate the surface of many plants, and can penetrate others only when the plants are weak, because they are growing in shade and moist situations when they need sun, or in dry conditions when they need moisture. Some plants are susceptible at any time to the fungi that like them.

There are three possible solutions to the problems caused by disease. You can select and grow totally resistant sorts of plant, which is the easiest, and in many ways the most sensible solution. You can also grow the susceptible plants so well that they are resistant to disease and, lastly, you can spray. Ideally, it is best to spray before the infection occurs, though this can be expensive and is always a bother. It's perfectly acceptable though, to spray roses once you've noticed blackspot, for the spraying will stop the fungus spreading, and once the infected leaves have dropped, your plants will look fine. Mildew on roses is tougher to get rid of, or on some varieties, even prevent.

Peach leaf curl is fairly easily controlled, but if it's prevalent in your area, spray in spring as the leaves expand.

Perhaps the most difficult disease to control is honey fungus, a soil-borne infection which attacks the roots of woody plants. It is sometimes called bootlace fungus, because of the black threads, or bootlaces, by which it spreads under the soil. There are special fungicides for treating the problem, but it is difficult to eradicate completely. Badly infected trees and shrubs are best burnt, and the site not replanted.

Always burn any infected wood, leaves, flowers or fruit. Left lying around, they will eventually produce more spores, and you will have more trouble.

Many shrubs and trees are affected very little by pests and diseases, but unfortunately one of our favourites, the rose, has more than its fair share and generally requires regular spraying during the growing season to keep it clean and healthy.

Pests

1 Birds *Various species do various sorts of damage – flower buds, particularly of forsythia, can be attacked, as can all sorts of ornamental fruit. You can protect vulnerable shrubs and trees, to a certain extent, with black thread strung over the branches, or use netting for wall bushes, scarecrows or cats.*

2 Blackfly *Some seasons these can ruin flowering cherries and much else. At the first sign of infestation, spray with malathion or derris, or simply pick off affected shoots and burn. Spraying is better if shoots are important for the plant's shape.*

3 Chafer beetle *This is a double pest, the grubs eating plant roots, and the adults feeding nocturnally – often on your rose buds in late spring and summer. Use a soil pest killer against grubs, if the infestation is bad. Spray roses with HCH (BHC) against the adults.*

4 Greenfly *These attack a wide range of plants, including roses. Most standard insecticides will kill them. Avoid using systemic insecticides on roses, especially single-flowered ones, which are popular with bees and hoverflies. Derris is best for these.*

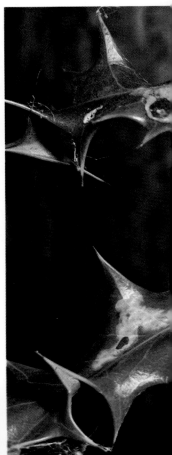

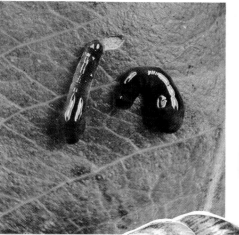

5 Holly leaf-miners *These can, occasionally, ruin holly bushes and hedges. The leaves develop unsightly blisters in the centre. At the first sign of infestation, pick off and burn the affected leaves. In bad attacks, spray the holly with dimethoate.*

6 Leaf-rolling sawfly *This pest is a particular danger to your roses, and it can strip the bush of leaves and buds. Look closely at any plant apparently late in leaf. Unroll any suspect leaves and inspect them; the sawfly grubs are pale green. Pick off rolled leaves and burn them.*

7 Slugworms *are the grubs of sawflies and feed on the upper surface of leaves. The best known are the rose slugworm, and the pear and cherry slugworm which is shown here. These pests are controlled by spraying with an insecticide such as malathion at the first signs of attack.*

8 Vine weevils *A dual nuisance, the adults eat oblong sections out of the leaf margins of many plants, rhododendrons, roses and vines. The grubs, which curl up if disturbed, eat the roots. Vine weevils can kill plants grown in tubs, especially hydrangeas. Dust the soil with HCH (BHC), or fork in a dressing of soil insecticide, to kill the grubs.*

9 Snails *These are not often a major problem for trees or shrubs, though they like hiding in bushes, especially box. Wall plants and climbers, such as clematis, can be attacked. Poison snails with proprietary slug pellets scattered round the base of the plant. Alternatively, an old-fashioned method is to catch snails at night (you'll need a torch) and sprinkle well with salt to kill.*

Diseases

1 Bacterial canker *This is occasionally seen on ornamental cherries, peaches and plums. Shoots or branches with prematurely yellowing leaves, later dying, are one symptom, and small, circular 'shot holes' on leaves in late spring are another. Remove and burn unhealthy wood. Spray the plant with Bordeaux mixture in autumn and spring.*

2 Blackspot *This fungal infection appears as dark, rounded marks on rose leaves from late spring onwards. Infected leaves soon drop. Remove and burn infected leaves. Spray plants, where feasible, with benomyl or captan.*

3 Honey fungus *Honey-coloured toadstools appearing at the base of tree trunks or shrub stems are a sign of honey fungus. If you peel away the bark, there will be whitish fungus, and black strands in the surrounding soil, which gives the disease its other common name, boot lace fungus. Try one of the commercial remedies, but it is difficult to cure and badly infected plants should be dug up and burned.*

4 Mildew *This first appears as whitish patches on leaves and flower buds, especially on some sorts of rose. The disease spreads rapidly, so spray with benomyl, dinocap or sulphur-based spray. Some plants attacked in damp conditions, others in dry.*

1

2

3
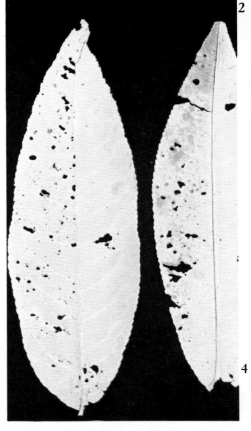

4

5 Peach leaf curl *On ornamental almonds, apricots and peaches, infected leaves become swollen and reddish. The disease can be fatal. Spray as the buds unfurl in spring with copper or sulphur-based fungicide, then again in a fortnight. Spray also in autumn just before leaf fall.*

6 Rust *Types of this fungus attack many plants feeding inside the leaves, later showing in summer as rust-brown pustules. Remove and burn infected leaves. If serious, prevent further infection by spraying with thiram or zineb at fortnightly intervals.*

7 Rhododendron bud blast *Infected buds die, and sprout black hairs the following spring. These contain spores. Remove and burn infected buds. The disease is spread by leaf-hoppers so, if practical, spray the plant with derris or malathion.*

8 Fire blight *A bacterial disease most likely to attack pear trees, but may also occur on ornamental shrubs such as cotoneaster and pyracanthus. In spring and summer, blossoms turn black and discoloration spreads to young shoots and along branches. Leaves hang down, blackened as if by fire. This is a serious disease and, if an outbreak is suspected, it should be reported to the Ministry of Agriculture.*

CHAPTER 5

SMALL SHRUBS

For sheer versatility, small shrubs are hard to beat and a selection of them will readily transform even the tiniest garden. Choose those that are suitable for the soil and the site – then sit back and enjoy the display.

These smallest of shrubs include some of the garden's most popular plants, and many of the most adaptable. All of them can play an important role in your garden, whether you have a 'pocket size' one, or something much grander. They can be used at the front of borders, to soften the edges of path or patio, or even to make exclusive but miniature gardens.

Some of the most charming small shrubs have the same habits and shapes as their larger relatives, so dwarf rhododendrons, dwarf conifers, and the low growing sorts of heather can be used to make tiny landscapes, in large tubs, earthenware troughs or old sinks. Old-fashioned white-glazed sinks are easily found in builders' yards. You can give them a stone-like appearance by coating the surface with a suitable glue and pressing a mixture of coarse sand and peat onto the glue. Most of your plants will like a free-draining, peaty soil, so make sure that the container has good drainage holes.

Mini-landscapes don't have to be in containers. They can look equally pretty in raised beds (useful, because all the plants are worth looking at closely), beside steps, at the edge of your patio, or as a rockery. Rockeries are difficult to do well, but if you do want one, try to make the stones look like a natural outcrop of rock, and tuck the plants in between in an equally natural way. Don't just scatter plants and stones at random over a pile of soil – it will never look attractive, and you will have wasted your money.

When planning mini-landscapes, it's often a good idea to have a larger shrub to provide a backdrop. If you are planting a raised bed, plant a shrub that will sprawl over the edge to give a less raw appearance. Many of the small brooms *(Genista* and *Cytisus)* can be useful in these situations.

Small shrubs are essential, too, at the front of shrub borders to give masses of low-growing colour. All the rock roses (the name covers plants of both *Helianthemum* and *Cistus)* are good for this, though they do need full sun. If your shrub border is in partial shade, try a shrubby *Potentilla* – they have flowers in creamy-white, yellow, apricot,

orange or red, according to cultivar. *Caryopteris* × *clandonensis* is another alternative. It's a plant that should be in every garden, and right at the front so that you can touch its fragrant leaves, as well as admire the clusters of soft blue flowers.

Small shrubs make wonderful 'softeners' for the edges of borders, especially when there's a path along the front. Masses of the silvery leafed cotton lavender *(Santolina)* look good spilling over brick or stone, as does the even more brilliant white curry plant *(Helichrysum italicum)*. Its leaves have an exciting spicy smell, though it's worth trimming off the flowers – they aren't especially interesting, and smell very much stronger. The various sorts of rock rose look equally effective, though some of the helianthemums have such brilliantly intense flowers that they need using with discretion. Try using different shades of the same colour rather than the strongest possible contrasts.

If you have a paved terrace or patio, and you find that the large expanse of stone or concrete looks a little 'hard', it's often worth removing a few sections of the surface (away, that is, from where you sit or walk), and planting up the space with some small shrubs. Good shrubs to plant in hard-paved areas include daphne (the glossy leaved *D. retusa* makes a low and attractive bush, filled with heavily perfumed flowers in late spring, and later hung with garnet berries) and the pretty 'herring bone' cotoneaster *(C. horizontalis)*. The berries of daphne are poisonous, so if young children use your garden, it is best not to grow them. If your patio is shady, plant a few of the evergreen and crimson-berried skimmias.

Elsewhere in the garden, it is always an attractive idea to have the paths actually hedged on either side. Cottage garden paths have always looked inviting when edged with lavenders (there are pink and white sorts as well as the softly coloured 'Munstead' or the intensely violet 'Hidcote') or variegated thyme. Cuttings of all of these root easily, so you only have to buy a plant or two to start with. If you like standard roses, try underplanting them in the same way –

Opposite *The rock roses or cistus, like C. crispus 'Sunset', are excellent front-of-the border shrubs for a sunny, well-drained position and will flower over many months in the summer.*

Opposite 1 *The low-growing barberry (*Berberis thunbergii *'Atropurpurea Nana') is ideal for edging or for forming a low hedge.*
2 *Ideal for the deepest shade is the butcher's broom (*Ruscus aculeatus*). It will also tolerate very dry soil.*
3 *The low-growing* Caryopteris × clandonensis *is a front-of-the-border shrub for full sun.*
4 Cotoneaster horizontalis *produces masses of flowers in early summer, much loved by bees, followed by red berries.*
5 *There are many dwarf conifers available; thujas especially make neat globular bushes.*
6 *There are also dwarf varieties of spruce or picea, which make suitable specimen conifers for a rock garden.*

an Elizabethan idea well worth copying. If you want something more modern, many of the small sorts of berberry also make good low hedges, especially in front gardens, but it's also worth trying Irish heath (*Daboecia cantabrica*) or some of the smaller sorts of spiraea.

If you like herbs, there are quite a number of small shrubby ones. There are lovely silver or gold variegated thymes, many sorts of marjoram, six or seven interesting types of sage, winter savory, hyssops with various flower colours, the lavenders, lad's love (*Artemisia abrotanum*) with its grey-green foliage, the small-growing sorts of rosemary, and plenty of others as well.

Most of them do excellently in window boxes or pots (don't grow thymes, though, in windy or exposed situations). However, if you've space, it is better still to have a herb garden. Although quite a few of the herbs you need for the kitchen are annual or herbaceous plants, the shrubby ones will provide the basis for the garden design, as well as giving you something to look at in winter. Edge the paths with hyssop (there are ones with pink or white flowers, as well as the usual – and lovely – blue sort), winter savory, or the various thymes.

If you do not have space for a full-scale garden, try a herb 'wheel'. These are sometimes made from an old cartwheel, placed flat on the ground and with a different herb planted in each of the sections between the spokes. If you don't want to use an old wheel (they rot after a year or two), it is just as easy to use bricks set on edge to make a similar design. The end result is often better looking, too.

Some of the most popular of all small shrubs include the vast numbers of heaths and heathers (from the two genera – *Erica* and *Calluna*). It's easy to have varieties in your garden that flower every month of the year, and as the varieties also have different growth habits and leaf colours, it's possible to have an interesting garden made from them alone. Most gardeners like to add a few dwarf conifers to get an extra bit of visual contrast. The only problem with heather gardens is that as all the flowers are pretty much the same shape and size, you might eventually feel like having something more exciting. Add some pernettyas or sarcococcas – the first for berries, the second for perfumed flowers. Heather gardens are often planted for 'low-maintenance', but even if that is what you want, it's important to watch out for the various perennial weeds, couch grass and convulvulus especially, that can establish themselves almost without your noticing and rapidly take over.

Recommended Shrubs

Barberry (*Berberis thunbergii* 'Atropurpurea Nana')
This lovely foliage and berry shrub does well in sun or shade, and on most soils. The leaves are a deep, coppery purple, the flowers orange, and the berries that follow, bright red. It makes a colourful 'accent' plant, especially in association with heathers. It's also a good 'edger'.

Broom (*Cytisus* × *kewensis*)
This marvellous hybrid has elegantly sprawling branches that vanish beneath sheets of creamy flowers. The spectacular display lasts for a few weeks in spring, but makes the plant essential to have. Broom needs full sun, but will do in most soils. It makes a wonderful edging to a path or a raised bed.

Broom (*Genista lydia*)
Another sort of broom, *G. lydia* is one of the best dwarf forms, with graceful, arching branches covered in intense yellow flowers in late spring and early summer. It is perfect for rock gardens and heather beds. It does well in almost any soil, though it flowers best in full sun.

Butcher's broom (*Ruscus aculeatus*)
An odd member of the lily family, this evergreen grows well in the deepest shade, and even in very dry soil. What look like leaves are flattened stems, and the tiny flowers produced on their surface later form long-lasting crimson berries. It is a tolerant shrub, good where little else will do.

Caryopteris (*C.* × *clandonensis*)
A tough shrub for almost any soil, caryopteris likes plenty of sun. The leaves are pleasantly aromatic. It can be cut back in late winter or early spring if you need to keep it small. The soft-blue flowers open in late summer and last into mid-autumn. It is good for a low hedge.

Cotoneaster (*C. horizontalis*)
Sometimes called the 'herring-bone' cotoneaster because of the regular arrangement of its side branches, it is a most attractive bush for rockeries, against low walls or even the house wall. The plant adapts itself to the shape of whatever it grows over. The leaves are small and glossy and the tiny flowers are followed by masses of berries.

Conifers
There are vast numbers of dwarf kinds. The dwarf cedar develops a short trunk, but its weeping branches are perfect for the rock garden. The thuja, a dwarf form of the

Opposite 1 *Heathers, like varieties of* Calluna vulgaris, *make excellent ground cover and flower over many months.*
2 *Lavender has many uses: plant it with old shrub roses, use it for edging a path, or plant it in a group by the front door.*
3 *There are few shrubs which have such a long flowering period as the potentillas. Most are dwarf compact shrubs, ideal for small gardens.*
4 *Rock roses (or cistus) are good companions for potentillas, needing the same sunny conditions and well-drained soil.*
5 *Rock roses (or helianthemums) are low spreading shrubs, ideal for rock gardens or dry sunny banks.*
6 *To obtain the showy berries on skimmia, plant groups of male and female plants together. Skimmia is also attractive when in flower.*

Chinese arbor-vitae, makes a small, globular bush, while the picea, or white spruce, will make a bright-green cone 2m (6ft) high in thirty years' time. Dwarf juniper will eventually give sheets of grey-blue leaves.

Cotton lavender (*Santolina neapolitana*)
There is another popular white leaved species (*S. chamaecyparissus*), but this one, with its longer, more feathery leaves, is the prettier. It makes an excellent shrub to sprawl over paths or paving. Cotton lavender is happy in poor soil, prefers full sun, and is exceptionally tough.

Curry plant (*Helichrysum angustifolium*)
This is an easy and attractive bush for sun or light shade. The narrow white leaves give off a pleasing curry smell when touched. The plant is happy in any free-draining soil. It is a good sprawler for patio or paths, or as an 'accent' plant among shrubs.

Daphne (*D. retusa*)
A gorgeous evergreen daphne, it eventually makes a dense, rounded bush. The leaves are oval and glossy, and the pale-lilac pink flowers, carried in mid-spring, will perfume the whole garden. They're followed by large, translucent, garnet berries.

Euonymus (*E. fortunei* 'Emerald 'n' Gold')
This popular shrublet, looks good planted with conifers and heathers, or as ground cover. Planted in the rockery, or against walls, the stems will climb and clamber. It's extremely tough, and does well in sun or shade. In this form the leaves are green, yellow and pink. Named forms like 'Silver Queen', and 'Colorata' which has purple tinged leaves in winter, are equally pretty.

Heaths and heathers (*Erica* and *Calluna* varieties)
Vast numbers of sorts can be found at most garden centres. All do well in moderately peaty soil and full sun. Use them in rockeries, or in a small bed. Gentians do well in similar conditions, and the wonderful blue flowers will give added interest.

Irish heath (*Daboecia cantabrica*)
A plant for loamy or peaty soils, it soon makes a handsome clump of glossy leaves and spikes of large, long-lasting, amethyst, purple, pink or white flowers. Clip over when finished. Useful to give height to heather beds, or to plant below rhododendrons and azaleas.

Lavender (*Lavandula* varieties)
These well known and much loved shrubs have fragrant leaves and fragrant flower spikes, often in various colours. 'Hidcote' is

deep purple, but others are paler, even pink or white. Lavender is lovely with 'old' shrub roses, or edging a path, or as bushes by doorways. Replace every few years with cuttings, as it tends to get leggy.

Potentilla (*P. fruticosa*)
There are many lovely, shrubby potentillas with arching branches and silvery, grey or green leaflets. For much of the summer, single flowers are produced, in white, cream and yellow, or even red, according to cultivar. Grow them in sun or partial shade, in rockeries, or as edgings.

Rhododendrons
While some species are tree sized, there are dozens of tiny sorts, all good in peaty pockets in the rockery, as part of the heather bed, or with azaleas (which are also part of the *Rhododendron* family). 'Pink Drift' is ideal for rockeries, with lavender-pink flowers. 'Yellow Hammer' is early and bright yellow. 'Moonstone' has fine reddish buds which open to palest yellow flowers. *R. sargentianum* is good for a cool shady place in the rock garden, with soft yellow to whitish flowers.

Rock rose (*Cistus* species and varieties)
These plants love hot, dry positions, so they're excellent in rockeries, or dry banks, or even in pots. No single flower lasts long, but they're produced in such abundance for much of the summer that it doesn't matter. They are good, also, for window boxes.

Rock rose (*Helianthemum nummularium* 'Fireball')
Fine for dry, sunny positions, even on poor soil, rock roses are fast growing. They are excellent for a rockery, pots on the patio, or at the front of the shrub border. 'Fireball' has exceptional double flowers, brilliant red, and in profusion for most of the summer. Look for other cultivars, too, with white, yellow, scarlet or pink.

Skimmia (*S. japonica*)
These compact evergreens have fine, glossy leaves and panicles of white flowers, often attractively fragrant. The form 'Wisley' is the easiest to grow, but you must buy male and female plants to get the splendid red berries that will last most of the winter. Shade and moist soil suit it.

Spiraea (*S. × bumalda* 'Anthony Waterer')
This is a good plant for almost any garden with plenty of sun. Prune hard in spring if you need a tidy-looking plant. As well as the flat bunches of crimson flowers in mid and late summer, the plant occasionally produces charming variegated shoots.

CHAPTER 6

MEDIUM-SIZED SHRUBS

The many medium-sized shrubs now available can provide autumn and winter colour, choice specimen plants or attractive fillers for borders and beds that will suit all conditions and will grace any garden, large or small.

Even if you have a tiny garden, it's important to include at least a few larger plants to give visual emphasis and a sense of scale. You have an immense range of lovely plants to choose from. Even if your garden is a bit larger, then you'll need medium-sized shrubs for the shrubbery, for 'specimens' to add interest to your lawn or patio, to make informal hedges, to use as large scale ground cover, or even to plant in tubs.

If you can only allow yourself one medium-sized shrub, look for one with several good points. *Mahonia aquifolium*, for example, has dramatic evergreen leaves, as well as sprays of wonderfully scented flowers in spring, and black berries in summer. Equally good are all the azaleas related to the popular *Rhododendron luteum*, most of which have heavily perfumed flowers and good autumn colours.

If you do have enough room for a shrub border, medium-sized plants are essential for their own sake, as well as making a good backing for all of the smaller sorts. Evergreen shrubs are especially important for giving 'body' to the shrubbery in winter, and stop the bare branches of the others looking too glum.

If you have room for some informal hedges, these can be used to screen off the compost heaps, the vegetable garden, or even the sand pit or swimming pool. Many sorts of barberry make wonderful hedging, offering attractive leaves, fine flowers (though sometimes with a nasty smell), often very colourful berries, and thorns too. Many other shrubs are quite as good, especially the upright sorts of rosemary. Fuchsias can be used for gorgeous hedges in warmer gardens, where they can become almost too large for this chapter. Also good value is the charming hypericum called 'Hidcote', smothered in shiny golden flowers from early summer into late autumn.

If you have room, it's fun to use some of the shrubs that have only one short flush of beauty before returning to the usual, and rather duller, state. A low hedge of the slow-growing and pineapple-scented mock orange, *Philadelphus microphyllus*, is a delight for the weeks that it is in flower. Try underplanting with the creeping plumbago *Ceratostigma willmottianum*, whose intense blue flowers will soon take over once the mock orange is finished, and will give you colour into the last days of autumn.

A wonderful hedge, too, can be made of the common daphne *(D. mezereum)*. To buy a hedgeful would be expensive, but once you've got a plant, it is easily increased from seed. The white-flowered form is the loveliest, though the smell of both, in early spring, is quite magnificent. The flowers are followed by good berries, amber after white flowers, scarlet after purple. Underplant with *Anemone blanda* if you want a spring display, or *Crocus speciosus* for wonderful flowers in autumn.

Many gardeners like to have some sort of specimen plant set in a lawn to offer a contrast to the flat green of the grass. If you have a small, grassed front garden, and really don't want a small tree or a really large shrub, there are plenty of grand medium-sized ones that will look good. Many sorts of *Pieris* look splendid, with their crimson or pink young leaves held in tufts at the end of each branch, soon followed by sprays of white or soft pink flowers. 'Firecrest' is a lovely form.

Abelia chinensis is another splendid specimen, not especially common and best in a rather sheltered site, but with soft-pink flowers in early summer, and a quite wonderful smell. The growth habit is fairly open, so you could easily plant bulbs beneath it – perhaps the intensely blue *Scilla sibirica* or one of the dwarf sorts of daffodil (*Narcissus asturiensis* is lovely).

Evergreens can make wonderful accents for a lawn, especially some of the narrowly pyramidal sorts. *Chamaecyparis pisifera* 'Boulevard' is good. They look better if you can group two or three, all of different sizes.

It's always difficult to decide exactly where a specimen plant (or plants) should go. If you buy containerized ones, shift them around to see where they look best. Alternatively, use some bamboo canes as dummy bushes. In general, the worst possible place for a specimen (except in the most formal of gardens) is in the centre of your lawn so try to avoid this.

Opposite *The hardy fuchsias are ideal medium-sized shrubs for gardens in milder areas, where they can be grown as specimens in a shrub or mixed border and the stronger-growing varieties as hedges, or as tub plants.*

Opposite 1 *The barberry (Berberis darwinii) flowers in spring, the blooms being followed by purple berries. It makes a particularly good informal hedge.*
2 *In full flower in late winter, Daphne mezereum likes moist soil and partial shade.*
3 *There are few better shrubs for autumn leaf colour than Euonymus alata and it grows particularly well on chalky soils.*
4 *An indispensable shrub for spring, Forsythia intermedia 'Spectabilis'. It will grow virtually anywhere.*
5 *The lace-cap hydrangeas, like 'Blue Wave', make a welcome change from the usual mop-headed kinds but also like light shade and moist conditions.*
6 *Japonica (Chaemomeles 'Rowallane') flowers in early spring and makes a good wall specimen.*

Another way of using shrubs as a 'feature' is to plant them in tubs, or very large pots. Good places to stand them are by doorways (not necessarily on either side), by flights of steps, in courtyards and patios, or to emphasize changes in direction of a path. The tubs must be big enough to let the plants grow properly, and will be too heavy to move around once planted, so move the empty tub from place to place until you've found exactly the right spot for it.

Tubs enable you to grow plants that wouldn't otherwise 'do' in your garden, and so you can try the lime-hating rhododendrons, azaleas and camellias (all three doing well with only the most basic care) however alkaline your soil. Another sort of shrub that does splendidly in tubs is the hydrangea, both the big showy 'hortensia' types and the subtler 'lacecap' ones. Almost any of the fuchsias look fine too, whether hardy or half hardy. An exceptional hardy sort with pinkish and variegated leaves is *Fuchsia magellanica* 'Versicolor'. If you have time, this can be cut to within a few centimetres (inches) of the soil in autumn, giving plenty of space to whatever bulbs you plant – some of the species tulips look wonderful. As the bulbs finish, the fuchsia begins to grow, and soon its lovely leaves and flowers tumble over the container.

Some medium-sized shrubs can even be used as large-scale ground cover – often useful in under-used parts of your garden. The laurel, *Prunus laurocerasus* 'Otto Lukyen' is particularly good, with glowing, deep-green leaves, and spikes of scented flowers in spring. A planting of this can look very good, and if you need some variegated foliage to make a particularly telling contrast, plant *Hebe* × *franciscana* 'Variegata'. Otherwise, use *Euonymus alata*, with its extraordinary autumn colour.

Another shrub which makes excellent large-scale ground cover is the mahonia (*M. aquifolium*), which is also known as the Oregon grape. It forms dense, suckering thickets of growth, effectively supressing most weeds. What is more, it is very adaptable, growing in sun or in shade, and in all kinds of soils, whether moist or dry. Often it is used for ground cover under trees. To keep it fairly low growing, it can be pruned back after flowering, but in this instance you will lose the purple berries, which are quite an attractive feature.

Some medium-sized shrubs are suitable for planting on very hot, dry banks, which can prove difficult for many plants. One of the best for this purpose is the rosemary (*Rosmarinus officinalis*), which has aromatic foliage, particularly noticeable in hot conditions. *Senecio greyi* would also be a suitable choice.

Recommended shrubs

Abelia *(A. chinensis)*
One of the less common shrubs, abelia is a relative of the honeysuckle. Good soil, full sun and a bit of shelter suit it. It produces clusters of small flowers, pale pink, much deeper in the bud, with an extraordinary perfume. It also does well in pots and tubs.

Azalea *(Rhododendron luteum)*
This lovely, loose-growing shrub, grows best in partial shade and peaty soil, but tolerates most other soils if you mulch. Wonderfully scented, luscious yellow flowers are produced in early summer. The leaves turn yellow and scarlet in autumn. Plant by your door, in a tub, or among other shrubs.

Barberry *(Berberis darwinii)*
Often voted one of the best of all shrubs, *B. darwinii* is good as a specimen shrub, in the shrubbery, or even clipped as a hedge. Evergreen, with handsome, prickly leaves, its sprays of soft-orange flowers are followed by purple fruits with a heavy 'bloom'. It tolerates any soil, preferably not dry, and in sun or shade.

Daphne *(D. mezereum)*
This easily grown daphne does well in most sites and soils. Flowers appear on leafless branches in late winter or earliest spring. They're in white or shades of purple, with a powerful fragrance. Attractive berries follow.

Euonymus *(E. alata)*
Not too common, but worth looking out for, one of the most splendid of all shrubs for autumn colour. Tolerant of almost any soil, it grows especially well on chalk.

False Cypress *(Chamaecyparis pisifera 'Boulevard')*
The species offers a good range of shrubs and small trees, this one a conical and neat-growing plant with silvery blue foliage. It makes an excellent specimen, though feed and water well. Lightly clip it if you need a particularly formal shape.

Forsythia *(F. × intermedia 'Spectabilis')*
'Spectabilis' is one of the best medium-sized forsythias, and deservedly popular. Branches disappear in a mass of yellow flowers in late spring. Any soil, full sun or partial shade suit it. If you'd like to try another colour, use 'Primulina', a lovely, pale yellow.

Fuchsia *(F. magellanica 'Versicolor')*
Often thought of as a foliage shrub, the

Opposite 1 *The dwarf laurel (Prunus 'Otto Luyken') is excellent for ground cover in shady areas.*
2 Mahonia aquifolium *looks good all the year round: purple berries follow the flowers.*
3 *One of the smallest of the mock oranges is* Philadelphus microphyllus, *with deliciously fragrant flowers.*
4 Pieris formosa forrestii *must have an acid or lime-free soil and a reasonably sheltered position.*
5 *Rosemary* (Rosmarinus officinalis) *is a culinary herb as well as a most attractive ornamental shrub for dry, sunny places.*
6 St John's wort (*Hypericum 'Hidcote') flowers throughout summer and into autumn.*

leaves are pink when young, grey green with cream variegations when mature. However, the flowers, crimson, add a touch of gaiety from midsummer onwards. It is excellent for tubs and pots, by steps or at the front of the border in sun. Any soil suits it.

Hebe (*H. × franciscana* 'Variegata')
An excellent foliage shrub, this hebe has leaves broadly margined in creamy white. Spikes of white flowers appear in summer. It grows in any well-drained soil, and is good for city or seaside gardens. It makes attractive informal hedges, and looks well combined with other evergreens.

Hydrangea (*H. macrophylla* 'Blue Wave')
'Blue Wave' is considered by many to be the finest of the lace-caps, which have a ring of large-petalled, sterile flowers surrounding a lacy mass of smaller fertile ones. It has strong, handsome leaves, and a graceful, low-growing habit. Feed and water well, and provide light shade. It is good for tubs or shaded courtyards.

Japonica (*Chaenomeles* 'Rowallane')
'Rowallane' is one of the best forms of this familiar plant, growing easily in most soils and sites. It is good as a specimen bush, can be clipped, or most splendidly of all, trained up a wall. The blood-red flowers are followed by speckled amber fruits.

Juniper (*Juniperus communis* 'Sentinel')
A pencil-thin variant of the common juniper, 'Sentinel' makes an excellent contrast to other plants in the rockery or heather garden, and makes a fine specimen plant, too. It does well in poor soil.

Laurel (*Prunus laurocerasus* 'Otto Lukyen')
A lovely, smaller form of the common laurel 'Otto Lukyen' has narrow, shiny leaves, held slightly upright. The spikes of white, heavily perfumed flowers are held well above the foliage, and appear in early spring. An excellent plant for shady courtyards or corners, it is very hardy, and not fussy about soil.

Mahonia (*M. aquifolium*)
Spiky leaves, purple or reddish all winter, long sprays of beautifully perfumed, pale-yellow flowers in late winter and early spring (worth bringing indoors), then rosettes of dark green new leaves, with strings of purple berries, makes this plant worthy of a space in any garden. It is happy in any soil, sun or shade.

Mock orange (*Philadelphus microphyllus*)
This twiggy bush with small greyish green leaves is fairly slow growing. It provides masses of delicate, white flowers with a magnificently rich scent that will fill the garden and grows to about 1.2m (4ft) high. It grows well even on poor soils.

Osmanthus (*O. heterophyllus*, syns. *O. ilicifolius, O. aquifolius*)
This is a slow-growing shrub of compact, rounded habit. It can be grown for hedging, in which case it will bear fewer flowers. Ideal for a scented shrub or flower bed, its clusters of white, fragrant flowers are borne from late summer through to autumn. The leaves are variable, some being similar to holly, while others on the same shrub may be spiny only at the tip. Though hardy, osmanthus needs shelter from cold winds.

Pieris (*P. formosa forrestii*)
A showy relative of the heather and rhododendrons, pieris likes the same sort of conditions, and looks splendid when planted with any of them. The young foliage is pretty, and masses of large, waxy, pale-pink flowers are produced in mid-spring.

Rosemary (*Rosmarinus officinalis*)
A lovely shrubby herb, rosemary is as essential in the kitchen as in the garden. Upright growing sorts make fine low hedges. Rosemary flowers prodigiously in late spring to summer, in shades of blue, pinkish, or white. Plant somewhere sunny, where you can touch it as you pass by.

St John's wort (*Hypericum* 'Hidcote')
An easily grown and exceptionally hardy bush, St John's wort is covered with bright-yellow flowers for much of the summer and well into autumn. The leaves, deep green, are more or less evergreen. It makes a good hedge. Site it carefully, because the flower colour sometimes clashes with other shrubs.

Senecio (*S. greyi*)
A popular, tough and easily grown silver-leafed shrub, senecio is rather sprawling but easily pruned. Any well-drained soil is suitable, but the shrub will grow best in full sun. Sprays of egg-yolk yellow flowers can be removed if they don't suit your colour scheme. Senecio is good in tubs, and at the seaside. Also listed as *S. × Dunedin* Hybrids or *S. paxifolius.*

Woolly willow (*Salix lanata*)
This attractive, spreading shrub has silvery-grey leaves after the yellow catkins have faded. It is particularly useful where you need to see something flowering in early spring – in a rock garden near the house, or by the edge of the patio, for example.

CHAPTER 7
LARGE SHRUBS

Deservedly a popular choice for the bigger garden, large shrubs also have a worthy place in quite small plans. Depending on the space you have available, you can opt for a wide-ranging display or a single, special show piece.

Among the large shrubs are some very aristocratic plants indeed, but ones which can look quite as 'at home' in tiny gardens as they do in vast ones. If you do have a small area, it's easy to reject them all as being far too big, but that would be a mistake. A single well-grown plant of, say, *Magnolia stellata* or the witch hazel *(Hamamelis)* or even *Choisya ternata* can absolutely make a garden, even if you have to restrict the other planting to accommodate it. Certainly, if your front or back garden is larger than 4 sq m (12 sq ft), it is essential to have something in this category.

In a very small space, use one of the wall shrubs. *Garrya elliptica* does well in shade, producing long silvery grey catkins in late winter, which last right through until the following summer. It's also possible to use *Choisya*, though it will try to sprawl forwards and you may need to fasten it up. It's certainly one of the top ten evergreens, with perfectly polished leaves of three leaflets, and clusters of white, perfumed flowers in spring and early summer. It looks very much at home in small paved courtyards, planted among ferns and periwinkles.

Against sunny walls, the possibilities are enormous. If you want something that perfumes the air in deepest winter, try the winter sweet *(Chimonanthus praecox)* with its waxy yellow flowers. Slightly showier are the so-called winter flowering viburnums. In fact, they flower from autumn through spring, but only during mild spells. Nevertheless, once your plants are big enough, you can cut a few sprigs with their groups of white or pink tubular flowers to perfume a whole room.

For summer flowers, there are so many lovely plants that will enjoy growing on a moderately sunny wall, that you will find choosing difficult. Many sorts of ceanothus are good – 'Gloire de Versailles' isn't too big, and its powder-blue flowers suit the skies of late summer. There are also large numbers of escallonias – all with a scattering of short tubular flowers, either white, every possible shade of pink or some fine, soft reds. Many of the also have attractive glossy leaves.

If you want berries for autumn, plant some of the pyracanthas – some of the yellow berried sorts are exceptional. Birds will often strip your crop before winter really sets in, so you may need to net the plants. Black nylon netting is less obtrusive than the bright green sort.

In larger gardens, large shrubs will play an important role – forming the most dramatic elements in the shrubbery. Use some for a burst of early summer flowers. All the lilacs are marvellous, from the simple elegance of the Persian sort to the gorgeous range of double-flowered ones. Dramatic foliage plants can be found too, including the dozens of sorts of the common elder *(Sambucus nigra)*, some with frilled or jagged leaves, others variegated with silver or gold, and perhaps the most splendid of all – the golden elder. This has red berries, so you will need another sort if you want to make properly coloured jelly or wine. Even the common privet has variegated forms, and these can make splendid fillers for the shrubbery if allowed to grow unchecked.

Of course, many large shrubs make good hedges too. Even sorts that don't take kindly to trimming can be used to make fine informal hedges. Almost any of the mock oranges *(Philadelphus)* are wonderful, and if you plant several varieties, you will be able to have flowers for most of early and mid-summer.

Several other shrubs included in this chapter also make very fine hedges. Escallonias, for example, make fine flowering informal hedges, and they are particularly recommended for gardens near the sea, although they will also grow inland.

If you want a berrying hedge, then choose one of the firethorns or pyracanthas. These are spiny, so will form an impenetrable boundary hedge. Usually the firethorn is grown as a semi-formal hedge, for if it is pruned too hard it will produce very few berries. The best time for light trimming is after flowering as then it is easy to see whether or not berries are being removed.

The golden privet (*Ligustrum ovalifolium* 'Aureum') also makes a very bright and

Opposite *The smallest of the magnolias is* M. stellata, *which flowers in mid-spring. Sun or dappled shade, shelter from cold winds, a good soil and plenty of feeding will ensure masses of gorgeous flowers each year.*

Opposite 1 *There are many varieties of butterfly bush* (Buddleia davidii), *a popular one being 'Royal Red'.*
2 *'Donation' is one of the best of the* Camellia × williamsii *varieties and flowers in early spring.*
3 *Suitable for seaside gardens, the deciduous* Ceanothus *'Gloire de Versailles'.*
4 *The peach-pink flowers of Escallonia 'Peach Blossom' appear in summer. It is an evergreen shrub, reaching about 2m (6ft) in height.*
5 *One of many good firethorns,* Pyracantha *'Orange Glow' is evergreen and attains about 4m (12ft).*
6 Garrya elliptica *makes a good wall shrub and the male catkins appear in mid and late winter.*

colourful hedge and should be trimmed regularly to produce a formal shape. It is a particularly good subject for town gardens. The problem with privet, though, is that it needs trimming several times during the growing season if it is to look neat at all times.

The place for the grandest shrubs of all, though, is somewhere that they can lord it over all your other plants – either as a specimen on the lawn, or rising above a bed planted with evergreen carpeters, bulbs or dwarf shrubs.

Earliest to flower is the witch hazel (*Hamamelis mollis*). The other species and varieties of witch hazel differ in flower colour and size – some being a showy, pink-stained orange. Alas, the showier sorts lack fragrance, and have thus lost the principal pleasure that the plant can give. The sort called 'Pallida' has pale lemon flowers and the strongest perfume – half almond, half rose. Later in the season comes the smallest of the magnolias, *Magnolia stellata*. The flowers (narrow petalled, bowl shaped, in white or palest rose) are borne in huge quantities, and a large bush in full flower is genuinely breathtaking.

Good for neutral or acid soils are the wonderful camellias. For some reason these are often thought of as difficult, though few really are. Not all have flowers that resist bad weather well, and others refuse to drop them when they're over, but some are amongst the grandest of all garden plants. The single sorts, the anemone-flowered ones, the semi-doubles and sumptuous full doubles· come in all shades of pink and scarlet, and most elegant of all, white. Many are veined, splashed or streaked in different shades. Some even have an elusive and delicious scent, though you really need to grow the plants in a cold greenhouse to fully enjoy it. One of the easiest of camellias, with wonderful drifts of orchid-pink flowers, is the lovely 'Donation'. It's a plant that every gardener should have.

The only disadvantage of large shrubs for modern gardens is that most of them take quite a few years to reach full size, and so to make their full effect. There are, though, some quick growing sorts. It's worth planting these in a new shrubbery, or wherever you need size quickly. Most of the large buddleias are excellent for this. Often called the butterfly bush, *Buddleia davidii* comes in various colours, from lovely white forms, to ones of the very deepest reddish-purple. Another good, quick and colourful plant is the broom *(Cytisus scoparius)*. Some have cascades of velvety scarlet flowers; others are pink and yellow or even rusty red. Perhaps the most spectacular of all is 'Cornish Cream' in just that colour.

Recommended Shrubs

Broom (*Cytisus scoparius* 'Cornish Cream')
This handsome shrub has closely packed, upright, whippy stems. From early to late summer, they are weighed down by masses of creamy white flowers. A quick-growing plant that likes full sun, and almost any dryish soil, it is particularly suitable for seaside planting.

Butterfly bush (*Buddleia davidii* 'Royal Red')
The graceful, arching branches in this cultivar are terminated by long trusses of unusual, red-purple flowers, which make an attractive background for the butterflies that will congregate in late summer. Prune the shrub hard in early spring to keep it compact and flowering well. Full sun and any soil are suitable.

Camellia (*C.* × *williamsii* 'Donation')
All camellias are wonderful shrubs for neutral or acid soils, either in open ground or in tubs. They have elegant, glossy leaves, a rather pendulous habit of growth and, in this sort, immaculate, semi-double pale-cerise flowers. Camellias do best against a sheltered wall, and are happy in sun or shade.

Ceanothus (*C.* 'Gloire de Versailles')
This handsome, rounded bush has bronzy green, strongly veined leaves. It flowers in late summer, producing spikes of a fine and delicate blue – though the framework stays behind and needs trimming back in late winter. Full sun and good soil are necessary, and it is a suitable plant for seaside gardens.

Escallonia (*E.* 'Peach Blossom')
A fine group of plants, escallonias are not fussy about soil or site, though some prefer shelter in winter. All are fine near the sea. Use them as hedges, windbreaks, wall shrubs, or single specimens. 'Peach Blossom' has bright pink flowers and particularly shiny leaves.

Firethorn (*Pyracantha* 'Orange Glow')
A splendid hedge or wall shrub, firethorn is very tough and vigorous. The white flower clusters are quickly followed by bunches of fine, orange–scarlet berries. The orange colour of this cultivar doesn't seem to attract the birds, so the berries are often safe until deepest winter. Any soil or site suits.

Garrya (*G. elliptica*)
Good against east or north facing walls, garrya is evergreen. The leaves can get

1

4

2

5

3

6

Opposite 1 *Plenty of space is needed for* Hydrangea paniculata *'Grandiflora', although it can be pruned hard to keep it more compact.*
2 Kerria japonica *'Pleniflora' flowers in spring, after which it is pruned hard.*
3 *The lilac called 'Sensation' has unusual flowers: purple-edged white.*
4 *The Mexican orange blossom* (Choisya ternata) *is pleasing all the year round with its evergreen foliage. It is hardly ever without flowers in spring and summer.*
5 *Most people think of privet only in terms of hedging, but the golden privet* (Ligustrum ovalifolium *'Aureum') makes a striking specimen in a shrub border.*
6 *A rather choice but easy winter-flowering shrub, ideal for wall training, is the wintersweet* (Chimonanthus praecox).

scorched by winter gales, though, so plant in shelter. Garrya is not fussy about soil or moisture levels, and is grown for its handsome male catkins, produced in mid and late winter. Female plants have long strings of berries in late summer.

Golden privet (*Ligustrum ovalifolium* 'Aureum')
The privets have a reputation for being boring, but when well grown make handsome shrubs. Golden privet can be hedged, but makes a spectacular specimen shrub, with brilliantly variegated, evergreen leaves. The flowers are perfumed. Very tough, golden privet prefers sun but will tolerate shade.

Hydrangea (*H. paniculata* 'Grandiflora')
If you want something really showy, this is it. The white flowers, carried in late summer, are immense 'mop heads', fading to dramatic tones of pale pink. Hydrangeas like a little shade and very rich feeding.

Kerria (*K. japonica* 'Pleniflora')
A useful and exceptionally tough shrub, kerria suckers so vigorously that it makes useful hedges and screens. The attractive, pom-pom flowers are orange-yellow. It is suitable for slightly wild gardens, under trees and to shelter more tender plants.

Lilac (*Syringa vulgaris* varieties)
These handsome, tree-like shrubs are best in full sun, but happy in most soils. Their perfume is a characteristic of early summer, and their trusses of spectacular flowers come in a multitude of shades of lilac, or in white. They can be single or double.

Magnolia (*M. stellata*)
An aristocratic plant, this magnolia likes a rich living – good soil, plenty of feeding, some shelter, and sun or dappled shade. It will reward you, once it's had a chance to grow, with a wonderful display of white or pale-pink flowers in mid-spring. Good plants to grow with it are ferns, ivy and white autumn crocuses.

Mexican orange blossom (*Choisya ternata*)
Happy in sun or shade, Mexican orange blossom likes a certain amount of shelter – the leaves can be damaged by icy wind. It appreciates feeding and moisture, but will do without. It has a splendid shape, aromatic evergreen leaves, and a thick scattering of scented, white flowers in spring and summer.

Mock orange (*Philadelphus* 'Avalanche')
Mock oranges do well even on poor soils, but do need sun. Out of flower, the form 'Avalanche' is upright and twiggy, clothed with neat leaves. In midsummer, the flowers are so abundant that the branches are weighed down in a very spectacular way. The flowers are single, white, and very heavily perfumed.

Red-barked dogwood (*Cornus alba* 'Elegantissima')
This dogwood is good in winter, when the thin, upright branches glow red among the other drab, brown shrubs. It is even better in summer, when clothed with narrow leaves, brilliantly variegated white and green. A good shrubbery plant and happy in most sites and soils.

Smoke bush (*Cotinus coggygria* 'Atropurpureus')
A splendid bush, its Latin name refers to the smoky purple plumes of tiny flowers and stems. It is pretty in the shrubbery or as an informal hedge. Try planting one behind small Japanese maples. The leaves have subtle autumn colouring, though for a more striking effect, try one of the purple-leafed forms, such as 'Royal Purple'.

Viburnum (*V.* × *carlecephalum*)
A 'high value' shrub, this viburnum is easily grown in sun on almost any soil. Its rounded clusters of white flowers appear in late spring, pink in bud, with a powerful and marvellous scent. The leaves are light green and attractively veined, often giving spectacular autumn colours.

Winter-flowering viburnum (*V. farreri*)
This will keep you out in the garden in midwinter, when its pink-budded, white flowers can perfume a sunny afternoon. The leaves are attractive, too, bronzy green and very nicely veined. Winter-flowering viburnum forms a picturesquely shaped bush, thriving in sun, or light shade. It tolerates most soils.

Wintersweet (*Chimonanthus praecox*)
This pretty and undemanding wall shrub is ideal if you've plenty of space on a sunny site, and don't mind waiting a few years before your shrub flowers. When it does, the small, yellow flowers will enliven winter with their very special scent.

Witch hazel (*Hamamelis mollis* 'Pallida')
This is a 'high value' shrub, though it lacks spectacular flowers. They are pale yellow, a bit spidery, but produced in midwinter and wonderfully scented. The leaves turn amber and yellow in autumn. A good 'specimen' shrub, witch hazel is happy in most soils, and will tolerate partial shade, if necessary.

CHAPTER 8

SMALL GARDEN TREES

For most people, no garden is complete without at least one tree somewhere in sight and, whether for decoration, for fruiting, or for foliage and bark effects, small garden trees seem to add an extra dimension to even the most grandiose layout.

It is possible to garden without trees, though trees are often what gives a garden its atmosphere. Even if your garden is tiny, look at it carefully to see where you could possibly fit a tree in – remember that all sorts of lovely plants will happily grow in the light shade of its leaves.

Trees can give your garden a sense of scale and serenity, can screen you from neighbouring properties, provide you with flowers in spring, shade in summer, and often good leaf colour in autumn. In winter, they can stop your garden looking too bleak and empty – some even have wonderfull bark to add interest to the winter scene.

Once you are convinced that you need a tree or two, it's tempting to be greedy and plant something fast growing – while promising yourself that you will cut it down when it's too big. However, by the time you notice that it's too big, it will probably be vast, and you won't feel able to tackle it. It is much better to plant something slower growing, which will remain reasonably in scale with your garden without too much work. Alternatively, use something moderately quick growing, but also easily pruned. The eating quince *(Cydonia oblonga)* is just such a plant, making a marvellous garden tree, its arching branches of silvery leaves covered with large flowers in spring. In autumn, the leaves turn clear yellow, and the branches are hung with amber quinces until you harvest them in early winter (they'll make the whole kitchen smell delicious).

If you like the idea of fruit trees in the garden, but don't want to encourage raiding parties of children, the quince is good but, if anything, the medlar is even better. It's quite slow growing (so you won't have to prune at all), but it eventually produces a very picturesque tree, ideal as a specimen tree on a small lawn. The flowers are large, creamy white, and held at the tip of every twig. The fruits are russet apple shaped – you should harvest them before the first hard frosts and store them indoors until they soften a few weeks later. Eat them fresh or turn them into delicious jelly. The leaves turn purple, bronze and red before

they fall, making it one of autumn's best sights. Its official name is *Mespilus germanica.*

The medlar has been almost forgotten as a fruit tree, but many gardeners still plant crab apples *(Malus* varieties). There are vast numbers of these, with fruit in all sorts of shapes and colours, though one of the best for both decoration and cooking is the popular 'John Downie'. The flowers are more heavily scented than most other apples, and they're followed by immense crops of oblong yellow fruits with a rosy flush. Jelly made from them is lovely.

The rowan *(Sorbus aucuparia)* has berries that are edible too, though if you want something more unusual than the wild plant's red fruits, look for some of the sorts with orange or yellow ones. *S.* 'Joseph Rock' has yellow fruit, *S. sargentiana,* scarlet. Birds, often being rather conventional, leave them alone until they're really hungry.

However, if you'd like a flowering tree (as opposed to one that fruits as well), there are hundreds to choose from. Laburnums are widely planted, but that doesn't stop them being wonderful to own in early summer, when they are decked out in yellow. Once your tree's big, plant a clambering rose beside it to grow up through the branches – laburnums are a bit dull when the flowers are finished. Never dull are the false acacias *(Robinia* species and varieties), and the drooping racemes of scented flowers are almost a bonus. The increasingly popular *R. pseudoacacia* 'Frisia' is grown for its golden foliage. It's worth growing by itself, or perhaps against something with dark-green leaves – an ivy-covered wall perhaps. Keep it well away from any other tree with coloured leaves, especially any of the purple ornamental apples or plums.

Some of these can look splendid elsewhere, though look for ones that have white flowers, or which flower before the leaves open. Two shades of pink on one tree can sometimes clash.

Amongst the flowering cherries *(Prunus* varieties) there are so many wonderful trees that you will wish you had enough room to plant them all. *P. sargentii* is perfect for a small front garden, but the winter-

Opposite *There is a very wide range of crab apples available and most are of a suitable size for small or medium-sized gardens. The spring flowers are followed by fruits, which in most varieties are highly decorative. The variety shown here,* Malus × eleyi, *is considered to be one of the most beautiful of all the crab apples.*

Opposite 1 *There are few small trees with better autumn leaf colour than the bonfire tree (Malus tschonoskii).*
2 *The crab apple 'John Downie' has the most colourful fruits of all, and they are edible.*
3 *Excellent for town gardens is the false acacia (Robinia pseudoacacia 'Frisia') with bright yellow foliage in summer.*
4 *The golden Indian bean tree (Catalpa bignonioides 'Aurea') can be grown as a tree or shrub.*
5 *The leaves of the golden sycamore (Acer pseudoplatanus 'Brilliantissimum') turn from pink to yellow-green.*
6 *The Japanese maple (Acer palmatum 'Osakazuki') has good autumn colour and attractive winter twigs.*

flowering *P. subhirtella* 'Autumnalis' is more easily found. In spite of its name, it flowers mostly during mild spells, and more abundantly near spring.

Sometimes it's useful to have a very narrow tree to give an 'accent' to a garden, perhaps by a path, or to make the corner of a boundary. Some of the evergreens do this exceptionally well. Not many gardens are warm enough to support the lovely Italian cypress *(Cupressus sempervirens)*, but there are several sorts of juniper that fulfill the same function. All are fairly slow growing, but can eventually reach 8m (25ft). To keep them in shape, it's worth putting a few twists of black twine around them in autumn, so that the snow doesn't build up on the branches and begin to bend them dangerously outwards.

Narrow forms of the flowering cherry have been very popular, though they almost always look tight and unnatural. They also get quite big. Try using instead one of the multitude of Japanese maples (mostly varieties of *Acer palmatum).* These are ideal small garden trees, often growing well even in very shaded gardens. New leaves are beautiful in youth and middle age, but all put on an extraordinary display of colour in autumn – though check the variety you're buying to see what colour it goes.

Many people, when they want a weeping tree, choose the weeping willow. This is generally a great mistake, for it eventually makes a gigantic tree, invariably swamping the entire garden. It is only, therefore, suitable for really large gardens.

Instead choose one of the small weeping trees, an excellent one being the willow-leafed pear (*Pyrus salicifolia* 'Pendula'). This is suitable even for small town gardens, and in spring and summer is most attractive with its narrow, silvery-grey leaves.

Trees are expensive to buy, and once they're established, are difficult to move, so place them carefully and plant well. Few small trees are particularly dangerous to house or wall foundations, but to be on the safe side, try to keep them 1.8m (6ft) away from danger areas. It's always pleasing to be able to walk underneath something, so plant one or two beside a path, beside the front gate or car entrance, or where they can shade a seat. Remember, too, that all trees help improve the 'townscape' if you live in a city, or the landscape in the country. Try to visualize how the tree will fit in with the location outside your own particular garden. In towns, the showiest and most colourful of trees can look excellent, though the same tree can look out of place in the country. In general, the best trees there are ones closely related to native species, or to kitchen garden fruits.

Recommended Trees

Bonfire tree (*Malus tschonoskii*)
This is a 'high value' small tree. It produces flower clusters in white or apple pink, followed by yellow–green fruits with a red flush. Most glorious of all in autumn, its leaves glow in flame colours. The bonfire tree is a good choice for a small, paved courtyard or patio, or as a lawn specimen. It will grow in most fertile soils.

Crab apple (*Malus* 'John Downie')
A handsome crab apple, 'John Downie' is slightly graceless in its winter shape, but is covered with heavily perfumed flowers in spring, followed by small oblong apples, rich golden yellow with a red blush on one side in autumn. They're delicious, but the birds clear them by early winter.

False acacia (*Robinia pseudoacacia* 'Frisia')
A very graceful plant with attractive furrowed bark in winter, this form has bright-yellow foliage in summer, as if in permanent sunshine. When it flowers, it does it tastefully, in white and yellow, and the flowers are fragrant. It is good in town gardens, and in most soils. It will also tolerate shade.

Golden Indian bean tree (*Catalpa bignonioides* 'Aurea')
The most dramatic of all the gold-leafed trees, this one has huge leaves, so plant it in a sheltered spot. Otherwise it is easy to grow, though it won't flower in colder areas. If you treat the plant as a shrub and cut it back annually, the leaves produced will be even bigger.

Golden sycamore (*Acer pseudoplatanus* 'Brilliantissimum')
This is a smaller, and special, form of the common sycamore. There are other yellow-leafed forms available, but this has very decorative young leaves, bright pink at first, turning yellow-green, then, for a short while, dark green. It needs sun and good soil, and regular feeding for best results.

Irish juniper (*Juniperus communis* 'Hibernica')
This lovely juniper is a very narrow-growing variant of the common juniper. It is very hardy and easily grown, even in poor soils. It is an excellent 'accent' in wild gardens, and essential in all formal ones.

Japanese maple (*Acer palmatum* 'Osakazuki')
A charming plant, the Japanese maple is interesting to look at even when leafless. The reddish buds produce jade-green,

1

4

2

5

3

6

Opposite 1 *The best of the laburnums is the form 'Vossii' as it has the longest flower trails of all. Laburnums grow particularly well on chalky soils.*
2 *Magnolia × soulangiana 'Alba Superba' can be trained against a wall if space is at a premium.*
3 *Not often thought of as an ornamental tree, the medlar (Mespilus germanica) makes a good lawn specimen and the leaves colour well in autumn.*
4 *The snowy mespilus (Amelanchier canadensis) is attractive in spring when it is covered in white flowers, and in autumn when the leaves change to brilliant hues.*
5 *The thorn (Crataegus prunifolia) has superb autumn leaves and berries and will grow in exposed and windy situations.*
6 *A far better choice for most gardens than the huge weeping willow is the willow-leaved pear (Pyrus salicifolia 'Pendula'). It makes a very shapely weeping specimen and is particularly suitable for urban gardens.*

lobed leaves. The colour lasts until autumn, when they turn almost laquer scarlet, and stay that way, for several weeks. It is happy in shade and good for courtyards.

Laburnum (*Laburnum × watereri* 'Vossii')
One of the grandest of the laburnums the form 'Vossii' is slow growing though eventually it makes a good-sized tree. In late spring, it is covered with immense trails of yellow, perfumed flowers. Being a sterile hybrid, it won't produce the poisonous seeds that are normally associated with laburnums.

Magnolia (*Magnolia × soulangiana* 'Alba Superba')
This magnolia is immensely popular, and justifiably so. It is best planted in rich, deep soil, never on chalk, and it does well in towns. It is a first class specimen tree, particularly if planted against a plain background. Large, perfumed flowers, perfectly white, appear in late spring.

Medlar *(Mespilus germanica)*
Medlar is a lovely and ancient fruit tree, of gnarled and picturesque appearance even when quite young. It carries showy, pale-cream flowers in early summer, and bronzed green foliage. In autumn, small russet fruits are produced, and the leaves turn purple, yellow and scarlet. Medlar is easily grown, and makes a good specimen tree.

Paper-bark maple *(Acer griseum)*
This is a 'high value' small tree, but in unusual seasons: autumn and winter. The leaves are orange, scarlet and red in autumn, and then in winter, the old bark peels away in sheets, revealing smooth, chestnut-brown bark beneath. It is very picturesque, easily grown, and is good as a specimen tree. Plant ivy or periwinkle beneath it.

Purple-leafed plum *(Prunus cerasifera* 'Pissardii')
This is probably one of the most popular purple-leafed trees with deep-red young leaves, turning purple as the season progresses. The flowers are white, though pink in bud. It is good in town gardens, or for a hedge, and easily grown.

Quince (*Cydonia oblonga* 'Portugal')
The quince is an ancient inhabitant of gardens. Its graceful growth habit is interesting when leafless; the young leaves are silvery, later dark green. Its handsome flowers are held above the foliage, like candles, and are white with a pink flush. The large, oval fruit is freckled in amber, brown and green, and is heavily scented. The leaves turn yellow in autumn.

Rowan (*Sorbus cashmiriana*)
A lovely small rowan tree, with many jagged leaflets to each leaf, it is very pretty even when not in flower or fruit. The flowers are whitish pink in clusters, and the fruits that follow are very large and white, like beads. They remain on the tree long after the leaves fall, and look very dramatic. It is easily grown.

Snowy mespilus (*Amelanchier canadensis*)
This pretty, twiggy plant makes a large bush or small tree, depending on pruning. A mass of tiny white flowers are produced in spring, before the leaves appear, and these are followed by edible berries. The leaves often colour wonderfully in mild autumns, and can be spectacular. It is very hardy and wind tolerant, and grows particularly well in damp soil.

Thorn *(Crataegus × prunifolia)*
This hybrid tree has purple twigs, handsome, glossy leaves, and the prominent cluster of flowers are followed by long-lasting, orange berries. These are wonderfully set off by the contrasting, scarlet autumn leaf colour. It is easily grown on most soils, and is excellent near the sea, or in similarly harsh environments.

Variegated holly (*Ilex aquifolium* 'Aureo-marginata')
This holly is often grown as a bush, but it is easily grown as a handsome tree. 'Aureo-marginata' has shiny green leaves in the familiar shape, but with an edge of cream. Excellent in town gardens, and easily shaped as you need, it can be allowed to grow to its full size in country locations. It is also good near the sea. The berries are a familiar red.

Willow-leafed pear (*Pyrus salicifolia* 'Pendula')
The willow-leafed pear is good for urban gardens and, as a specimen tree, it's often seen in 'white' gardens. A graceful, silver-leafed, weeping tree, it makes all sorts of colour schemes possible. Surround it with old roses, and lavenders, or twine clematis up through it. It is happy in most soils and prefers sun.

Winter-flowering cherry (*Prunus subhirtella* 'Autumnalis')
This cherry has rather small flowers compared to some other flowering cherries, but it is valuable because of its flowering season. In spite of the name, there is most flower in early spring. The leaves can colour well in long slow autumns. It is easily grown in most fertile soils but prefers a sunny location.

CHAPTER 9
CLIMBERS

In every garden, use can be made of vertical space by growing a few climbing plants. A combination of flowering and foliage kinds will enhance the walls of a house, but climbers can also be grown up pergolas and arches or through old trees.

All the climbers are immensely useful plants, and there can be no garden that isn't improved by having at least one or two of them. There's no reason why any gardener should have to look at an ugly wall, when it can be a source of great pleasure if covered with Virginia creeper (Parthenocissus quinquefolia), one of the hundreds of sorts of ivy (mostly Hedera helix), or even the climbing hydrangea (Hydrangea petiolaris). Climbers are perfect for small, city gardens which are surrounded by high walls, and where there isn't really room to plant some of the larger wall shrubs. Few climbers are ever thicker than 15cm (6in), so the wall can be entirely green while hardly reducing the ground area of the garden.

It's always worthwhile using several sorts of climber, if there is room. A large wall of one plant can get dull, but if there are several shapes and colours of foliage, you will find that they make a much better background for your other plants. Even if you can't provide some sort of support, there's still an exciting range of self-clinging climbers to choose from. All the ivies are good, whether you plant the spiky 'birds foot' ivy (H. h. 'Caenwoodiana'), or some of the handsome variegated sorts. Even that doesn't exhaust the ivy's range, for some types have leaves almost as frilled as parsley, others have elaborately jagged ones. When buying, make sure that the ivy is suitable for climbing – some are better for ground cover, or even small bushes.

Ivies are evergreen, but some of the deciduous self-clinging climbers are valuable for handsome summer foliage and dramatic autumn colours. The well-known Virginia creeper is deservedly popular, but try combining it with its pretty relative Parthenocissus henryana, or Boston ivy (P. tricuspidata).

If at all possible, add the climbing hydrangea to the other creepers. This gets off to a slow start, but grows fast once it gets started – and is worth waiting for. The autumn leaf colour is a lovely clear yellow which combines well with the scarlet and bronzes of the Parthenocissus species.

If you can provide wire supports or a trellis for your climbers, your range expands enormously, though on the whole most of the new possibilities need more sun than the self-supporting types.

Russian vine (Polygonum baldschuanicum) and Clematis montana are only suitable for the largest walls, and both can quickly swamp a small house. Even some of the honey-suckles can be quite rampant – though their luxuriance is a good part of their charm, the trumpet-shaped flowers the rest. If you choose your plants carefully, you can have them flowering from early summer well into early winter.

It's fun to have something a little bit grand against your house walls. All the summer-flowering clematis are lovely, though there are some extremely attractive, spring-flowering species. Sadly, the two sorts need to be pruned in different ways, so it isn't possible to plant them together, though the spring sorts can be combined with the summer-flowering solanums or with jasmine.

Some clematis are scented but common jasmine (Jasminum officinale) pours out its scent. Try growing it around doors or windows – cottages often have a wirework or wrought iron porch wreathed in masses of it. In slightly grander gardens, try making an 'arbour' – a spacious framework large enough to take a few chairs and a table – and covering it with jasmine. It will soon become a perfect place to spend a warm summer evening.

For south-facing house walls, at least in the warmer parts of the country, it's possible to get good crops of grapes. White sorts are usually easier than black ones, and check that you have an early variety. The leaves of most dessert types generally go amber-yellow in autumn, but the wonderful 'Brandt' goes scarlet (the fruit is black, small and very sweet), and Vitis vinifera 'Purpurea' has wine-purple leaves in summer, turning bronze and crimson in autumn. Both are very much worth growing, though in colder areas they won't actually produce a crop.

Even more than with other garden plants, with climbers it's important to think about

Opposite *The hybrid clematis, such as 'Hagley Hybrid', are summer-flowering climbers which can be trained to walls, fences and even through trees and large shrubs. All clematis appreciate cool roots and these should be shaded, with their top growth exposed to the sun.*

Opposite 1 Akebia quinata *is not one of the hardiest climbers and needs a warm sheltered wall.*
2 *The vigorous Chilean potato tree (Solanum crispum 'Glasnevin') can be pruned fairly hard if it outgrows its allotted space.*
3 *The Chinese Virginia creeper (Parthenocissus henryana) will succeed on a north-facing wall, and although vigorous can be trimmed to keep it within bounds.*
4 *Producing small flowers, but plenty of them, is* Clematis montana 'Elizabeth'.
5 *Large-flowered clematis include the well-known* 'Mrs Cholmondeley', *vigorous and easy.*
6 Clematis *'Ville de Lyon' produces large blooms from midsummer to early autumn.*

the flower colours. Against old stonework or old brick, or against weatherboard or wooden shingles, almost any colour will look good. However, it can be difficult to choose good colours to set against new red or orange brick, or even Victorian red brick. Colour-washed rendering can also be difficult. Against red brick, only the palest colours, or white, look at all right. One of the most floriferous of the white-flowered climbers is the lovely *Solanum jasminoides* 'Album', which stays in flower for most of the summer. It is actually related to the humble potato of the vegetable garden. Hard winters can cut it back, so protect the lowest parts of the stem with straw or sacking. White wisteria can look good but, on the whole, it's safer to go for foliage climbers. Try some of the *Vitis* or *Parthenocissus* species. Avoid anything variegated.

Pink rendered wall are only slightly less difficult, though flowers in other shades of pink can look nice. Pale, bleached-out colours that you might not consider for the rest of the garden can also work very well.

There's no problem at all with climbers in the garden itself, where almost everything looks perfect. Apart from climbers over arches, pergolas or fences, it's a good idea to use climbers over other plants – and if you choose species with different flowering times, you can have a long season of colour from a small area of ground. Some clematis look lovely scrambling through shrubs, particularly through some of the larger bush roses, or through old fruit trees. Ivies grow up trees in nature, and the garden forms can look really fine on the trunks of garden trees. The climbing hydrangea can look better still, though it needs a fairly substantial tree. If you don't mind a picturesque tangle (some gardeners are dreadfully tidy), the vines look splendid when allowed to twine upwards through a wall trained rose, and the autumn colours take over from the last of the flowers.

Sometimes, when gardeners cut down a large tree, which may have died, they are unable to remove the stump of the lower part of the trunk. In this instance, it is worth growing a suitable climber over it as camouflage. Several are suitable, especially the evergreen ivies or any of the honeysuckles.

Some climbers can even be grown without supports, being used as ground cover to clothe banks as an attractive alternative to grass. Clematis can be used in this way, particularly the small-flowered kinds such as *C. montana* varieties. Most of the ivies can also be used in this way and are ideal for shady banks. When buying ivies for such use, make sure you buy those sold as ground cover, and not those trained to canes.

Recommended Climbers

Akebia (*A. quinata*)
This lovely, almost evergreen climber can reach 9m (30ft) in height. The leaves, like a hand, are made up of five leaflets, oval and dark green. Against a south-facing wall, it will also have purplish, fragrant flowers in spring, and in a hot year, exotic looking fruit.

Chilean potato tree (*Solanum crispum* 'Glasnevin')
A fairly tough and hardy climbing potato, it is good for walls, low fences, even sheds and garages. Clusters of nightshade-like flowers in soft purple with a yellow centre bloom all summer and early autumn. It does best in full sun, but tolerates any soil.

Chinese gooseberry (*Actinidia chinensis* 'Aureovariegata')
This climber has stems covered with red bristles, producing dramatic and quite large variegated leaves, often of three colours. It likes sun and rich soil, and will produce both whitish yellow, fragrant flowers and fruit (the familiar 'kiwi' – though if you plant seeds from bought fruit you won't get variegated leaves).

Chinese Virginia creeper (*Parthenocissus henryana*)
This climber produces clusters of sticky discs to help itself up your walls. The leaves are very handsome, composed of several leaflets. In shade, the leaf veins are distinguished and pale. In all situations, the leaves turn wonderful reds in autumn. Fruits, if you're lucky, are blue. It is an extremely vigorous plant.

Clematis (*C. montana* 'Elizabeth')
'Elizabeth' is an attractive, pink-flowered variant of the species. It is slightly less vigorous, which makes it more useful, and slightly more fragrant. Good in most situations, but in a sunny one it will produce a sheet of flowers in spring and early summer. It can be pruned after flowering.

Clematis (*C.* 'Mrs Cholmondeley')
This is an excellent plant, vigorous (they aren't all) and easy. It produces hosts of elegant, pale-blue flowers, its petals quite narrow, giving a more delicate effect than some other large-flowered clematis. It is excellent for training along fences or around windows.

Clematis (*C.* 'Ville de Lyon')
This flowers best against a south facing wall, but grow among other plants, so that the lower stem and roots are shaded. Cut back, if you want, in late winter. Otherwise

Opposite 1 *One of the earliest honeysuckles to flower is the early Dutch (*Lonicera periclymenum *'Belgica').*
2 *Many varieties of ivy (*Hedera helix*) have variegated foliage, like the popular 'Goldheart'.*
3 *The summer jasmine (*Jasminum officinale*) will rapidly cover a wall or fence.*
4 *Although the vine (*Vitis vinifera *'Brandt') produces fruit in a good summer, it is grown primarily for autumn leaf colour.*
5 *The Virginia creeper (*Parthenocissus quinquefolia*) will rapidly cover a house wall and is self-clinging. Brilliant autumn leaf colour is its main attraction.*
6 *Regular pruning is necessary for wisteria (*Wisteria sinensis*) or it will produce a tangled mass of growth.*

allow it its head, and get earlier, and higher, flowers. It looks lovely scrambling among big roses or up old fruit trees.

Climbing hydrangea (*H. anomala petiolaris*)
The lovely chestnut-brown stems make nice patterns when leafless, the leaves are fresh green and glossy. Heads of creamy white flowers stand out from the main vegetation. It is perfect for north-facing walls, or up bare and boring tree trunks. It is an easy plant to grow, but slow at the start.

Early Dutch honeysuckle (*Lonicera periclymenum* 'Belgica')
This is a selected form of the lovely native woodbine, familiar in hedgerows and cottage gardens. 'Belgica' begins flowering in late spring and early summer, then flowers a little more in early autumn. Its flowers are reddish on the outside, fading to deep cream. It is a vigorous and very fragrant plant, suitable for sun or shade.

Ivy (*Hedera* varieties)
All the ivies are excellent and versatile garden plants, happy in sun or shade. All the sorts listed here are good for walls, tree trunks, over rockeries, or even over bare ground if you need ground cover. Ivies do well on most soils, and thrive in the best and worst corners of a garden.
H. helix 'Caenwoodiana' has rather small leaves, divided into three to five, narrow spiked lobes. It takes a while to cover fully, but is exceptionally graceful.
H. helix 'Gold Heart' has attractive leaves, each a glossy, dark green with three pointed lobes and a prominent spash of gold at its centre.
H. colchica 'Dentata Variegata' A most spectacular ivy, it has large, variably shaped leaves, green and greyish green, with a dramatic cream margin. It can be difficult to get started, but soon grows away fast.

Japanese honeysuckle (*Lonicera japonica* 'Halliana')
This very vigorous climber has evergreen leaves in shelter or warmth, but it loses its leaves in severe winters or exposed gardens. The flowers start in early summer and finish in midwinter. They are white, becoming creamy orange. Although the flowers are a little sparse, they are deliciously scented. Good for cutting.

Jasmine (*Jasminum officinale*)
The immense popularity of this climber is due to its pure-white flowers, overwhelmingly scented, in mid to late summer. It needs full sun, a little shelter, and rich soil. Easy and very vigorous, it is also good for growing in pots.

Jasmine nightshade (*Solanum jasminoides* 'Album')
A slightly tender climber of great beauty, it grows best against sheltered, south-facing walls. Give protection to the base of the stems in winter. It is covered with graceful, white, bell-shaped flowers all summer and until the first frosts. Vigorous, it happily grows up to 7–8m (20–25ft). Take summer cuttings as an insurance.

Russian vine (*Polygonum baldschuanicum*)
A quick growing and wildly rampant climber, it has coarse and undistinguished foliage. Russian vine is quite pretty in summer, when covered with sprays of small cream flowers. The plant will swamp sheds, garages, even small houses and trees. Good for quick cover, it creates problems when big.

Vine (*Vitis vinifera*) 'Brandt'
This popular, hardy vine is vigorous, growing up to 10m (30ft). It can fruit against a south-facing wall in a good summer. The blue-black fruit is both interesting and delicious, but the vine is primarily grown for the leaves – handsome in summer, dramatic as they change to scarlet and purple (the veins stay green) in autumn.

Vine (*Vitis vinifera*) 'Purpurea'
This is another dramatic vine, worth growing near 'Brandt', or mixing with a clematis or training up a silver-leafed tree. The leaves are red, then deep purple, finishing bronze and scarlet. The fruit, if you get it, is black and sweet. It thrives in good soil and plenty of sun.

Virginia creeper (*Parthenocissus quinquefolia*)
This familiar climber is still often seen covering Victorian houses. It is a vigorous climber, doing well in most soils and on most walls. Keep it trimmed if it endangers your gutters or windows. Virginia creeper provides wonderful autumn colours.

Winter jasmine (*Jasminum nudiflorum*)
This wall shrub should be in every garden, for it is very hardy, will grow almost anywhere and is happy even against a sunless north-facing wall. Growing to about 3m (10ft), its bright yellow flowers are produced from autumn to spring.

Wisteria (*Wisteria sinensis*)
One of the most artistocratic of the climbers, vigorous but not swamping, wisteria needs full sun, good soil, and some pruning to be at its best. In flower, it's worth all the work. Try it on walls, or if you've nothing suitable, on pergolas, up trees, or even as a standard.

CHAPTER 10

ROSES

Roses are so diverse in habit that there is one to meet almost every garden need: they can combine with other shrubs, fit formal bedding schemes or even make good hedges.

History

Gardeners seem to have loved roses almost since gardening began, and some sorts have been in cultivation for at least five thousand years. In Europe, by Greek and Roman times, though there were only a few rose varieties, they were already the epitome of beauty and luxury. Their flowering season was still very short, so roses were actually forced – to give rich Romans their pleasures a few weeks earlier. One Roman emperor of unusual tastes drowned his guests in rose petals at the end of a particularly good orgy. It's difficult to know what varieties he used, but several still grown are sufficiently old – including the so-called Jacobite rose *(Rosa alba maxima)* and the equally fine centifolia rose – to have been possibilities.

By Elizabethan times, British gardeners had quite a number of fully double roses, from the ancient and striped 'Rosa Mundi' to the absoutely lovely 'Empress Josephine' also known as 'Francofurtana'. Elizabethan gardeners also had rather more of what they called 'musk' roses, but they also liked briars, including the scented-leaf eglantine *(Rosa rubiginosa)*, and the double field rose. All had medicinal uses.

The passion for roses developed at the same time as more and more sorts of rose were brought in from the Middle East, India and China, and though no-one knew anything about sophisticated breeding mechanisms in plants, exciting new sorts began to appear. By the end of the 18th century, lovely new varieties appeared every season, mostly fully double, in white or in subtle shades of pink. All were marvellously scented but had (with one exception), a short flowering season of three to four weeks in midsummer.

The 19th century, with the gardening world now fully aware of the possibilities of plant breeding, was poised to make use of the China rose. This ancient Chinese garden plant (still worth growing in its own right) flowers throughout the growing season, and new, long-season roses soon appeared, still in the 'old' colour range. Though the yellow flowered Austrian briar, *(R. foetida)* had been in gardens here for centuries, in the latter part of the 19th century it was crossed with some of the new 'perpetual' roses to give a completely new series of shrill reds, oranges and, most exciting of all, fully double yellows. The Austrian briar also allowed an obscure fungus – black spot – that attacked it to attack all its progeny.

With more and more species still arriving, and more breeding taking place, nursery catalogues listed thousands of roses. The tea scented rose *(R. × odorata)* arrived in 1810, but took fifty years before it, too, was crossed with the new sorts of rose. It produced the hybrid tea roses, which soon became so popular that all the other sorts or rose, however lovely, were almost instantly dropped. It's gone on to become almost the rose of the 20th century.

Classification

Nothing in the rose world stands still. Most sorts of rose cross with most other sorts, so no sooner does one classification become established than the groups of roses it defines dissolve or vanish as breeders get to work. None of this stops roses, old and new, being any less beautiful – but the present classification is more or less as follows:

Wild roses This group includes all the basic species (though remember that some of these are not true species, found in the wild, but simply ancient garden plants that have been given names like *R. damascena, R. alba* etc.). It also includes the varieties of wild and garden species, as well as some of the simplest crosses between them. Thus the lovely 18th century Alba shrub rose 'Céleste' finds itself here, as does the modern 'Nevada', derived from *R. moyesii*. There are dozens of wonderful garden plants, from immense climbers that will produce shoots 8m (25ft) long in a season, right down to dwarf forms of *R. chinensis*.

Old garden roses These comprise the many roses, mostly fully double and with short flowering seasons, that were in gardens before 1860, the date that marks the advent of the hybrid teas. Over the last thirty or forty years they have become newly fashionable as some gardeners have turned away from the strong colours and sometimes poor perfume of hybrid teas and polyanthas.

Opposite *One of the most popular groups of roses are the cluster-flowered or floribunda roses, which are ideal for mass planting in beds. The variety shown here is 'Dearest'.*

They've rediscovered some wonderful plants – and as old garden roses rarely need pruning, they rather suit gardeners who are busy and don't insist on colour all summer. Ironically, some breeders have started crossing the best of the old types with modern ones – in the hope of getting perpetual flowering roses with the old shape, colour and scent. Some of the results are very pretty and do have a long season, but have (so far) lost a little of the finesse of the old sorts.

Modern garden roses The Victorian passion for bedding schemes needed plants that flowered all summer. The hybrid tea, easily pruned and kept as a small bush, fitted their ideas perfectly. The colours, once the Austrian briar had been mixed in, were strong, rich, or at least cheerful (none of those anaemic pinks of the previous generation). Many gardeners still like rose beds, and the hybrid teas are still ideal. They're now assigned to a sub-group called large-flowered bush roses, and have elegant buds, opening into flamboyantly large flowers.

Plants with small leaflets and bunches of small, rosette-shaped flowers comprise the polyantha group, and also contain many roses especially suitable for bedding.

Tall-growing roses, classed as ramblers or climbers, recruit roses from all classes. Some are simply climbing 'sports' (a sort of minor mutation) of hybrid tea varieties, others are hybrids between rampant species (like the musk rose) and various sorts of bush rose, and others are closely related to, or exactly the same as, wild species. Some can be used on house walls, on pergolas and arches, or even to climb up trees. If you have a large-scale wall, try covering it with *R. brunonii* 'La Mortola' or *R. filipes* 'Kiftsgate'.

The miniature roses are largely developed from the dwarf form of the China rose. They're exceptionally pretty, though they are difficult to integrate into the general garden – their refinements are rather lost if planted with other small shrubs. They do well in large pots, and that's probably the best way of actually *seeing* them.

However, don't worry about rose groups too much. It is some help in knowing how to prune – though that's most important for the bedding roses – but if you begin to explore some of the tens of thousands of marvellous roses now available, you'll be too excited to care.

Growing roses
Buying
If you want a few colourful bushes for a rose bed, have a look at what your local garden centre sells. Wait until flowering starts; that way, you can see exactly what the flowers are like, and also check that the plant is properly established in its container. It is best to choose plants with a few strong-growing shoots, with good bark and leaves, rather than one with a greater number of scrawny stems.

However, no garden centre can hope to carry anything like a representative selection of this vast group, so you're unlikely to find anything much outside the three or four dozen most popular plants. If you need something unusual, you'll almost certainly have to buy from a specialist nursery. If at all possible, visit it during the season – you might see roses even more beautiful than the ones you initially wanted. If you can't visit in person, get your order in as quickly as possible once you've read the catalogue.

Your roses will arrive bare rooted. It's almost always worthwhile giving the roots a soak in a bucket of water for a few hours as soon as they arrive. In the unlikely event of your plants arriving badly shrivelled, bury the plants in a trench in the garden for a week or so.

Planning
If you want proper rose beds, remember that maintenance is much easier, the simpler the design. It's best to have the rose beds in an open part of the garden, rather than against a wall or fence. Beds should be about 1.5m (5ft) wide, which will allow you to plant bushes three deep, and still give yourself 30cm (12in) between the outermost rose and the edge of the bed. That's enough to avoid too much overhang, which can make mowing, weeding and even walking past difficult. The paths between the beds need to be at least 1m (3ft) wide. If your design needs height to make it look exciting, plant standards in the centres of the beds, or plant ramblers up a tripod of poles.

Colours can be problematical. Unless you are keen to look at lots of different varieties of bloom, plant simply. A bed with every rose a different variety often ends up looking a mess. One famous rose garden is planted up in white and different shades of yellow – and looks wonderful.

Don't forget that you don't *have* to prune rose bushes. Quite a number of hybrid teas or cluster flowered sorts make perfectly respectable shrubs, and can simply be added to the rest of the garden. 'Iceberg' and 'Allgold' are particularly good.

All the proper shrub roses do well in the general garden. Watch colours, though. Don't try to combine 'old' roses with modern sorts, because they'll clash badly. Do plant old roses with silvery leafed shrubs and herbaceous plants, all sorts of herbs, especially sages, lavenders and

Below *Roses may be supplied bare-rooted, in which case planting should be carried out between autumn and the end of early spring.*
Bottom *Many garden centres sell roses in containers, in which case planting can take place at any time, provided the ground is not frozen or waterlogged.*

thymes, and always where you can easily reach them. A garden seat with a bush of 'Ispahan' or 'Fantin Latour' on one side, and an eglantine rose on the other, will be the favourite one in the garden. Alternatively, plant shrub roses by doorways, under windows, along paths, or surrounding the edge of a patio.

Climbers and ramblers look good on tripods, house walls, pergolas, arches or screens. In small gardens, choose perpetual-flowering sorts, unless you're perfectly happy with one burst of splendour or are prepared to plant other climbers as well.

Planting
Autumn is the best time if you can manage it – order early. The end of early spring is about the latest for bare-rooted plants. Roses give you back what you give them. Prepare their quarters well, and when planting, add a bucketful of peat mixed with a handful or two of bonemeal for each plant. Check for any developing suckers, dead and damaged roots and shoots. Most of your roses will be budded, and the union of stock and scion should be just below the final soil level.

If you are planting bedding roses, the average distance between plants is 45cm (18in), but some vigorous types such as 'Peace' need 60cm (2ft). Standard roses need to be staked at planting, so make sure that you have suitable posts to hand.

If you have spare rotted manure or compost, give the new plants a good mulch. It's helpful if you can get them to do well in the first season.

Pruning
New plants may have been pruned before they were sent out. Otherwise, once you have got them planted, clear out weak twiggy growth and prune bush roses hard, then leave well alone. In subsequent seasons, if pruning is needed, try to prune between midwinter and early spring.

How you prune hybrid teas depends mainly on your garden soil. On rich heavy loam, prune hard. Remove all but three of the main stems, shortening those to about 15cm (6in), and to an outwards-facing bud. On light, sandy soils, give only a light pruning. Do this by removing weak growth, and shortening the remaining stems by a third. Gardeners gardening on light soil who like their hybrid teas grown low, will find they need to keep their plants well fed and watered.

Floribundas need more work; new shoots that grew from the base of the plant last summer are clipped back to any bud just below the old flower truss. It will go on to produce flowering side shoots – these are shortened by half in the subsequent winter. The shoots later produced by those trimmed side shoots are cut back hard in the third winter, leaving just two or three buds. Meanwhile the plant has produced second and first season shoots for you to prune.

You can leave most of the shrub roses ('old' ones included) almost entirely alone. Some occasionally produce a few very fast-growing shoots and these can look ungainly. Simply shorten them. Others have rather pendulous growth, and if the stems get long the bush falls apart. Either shorten or, better still, build low supports of lath to hold the flowers up where you can see them.

Some 'wichuraiana' hybrids need treating like raspberries, in that canes produced one year flower in the second, and are then cut out. Most other ramblers and climbers can be left to their own devices, except to remove dead or inconvenient stems. In others, all new growth may go to the tips of old stems, and the plant become leggy and bald lower down. Stems of these can be induced to bud and flower along their length by training them horizontally or fan-wise. In general, though, most ramblers and climbers will give you plenty of flowers if you feed them well, watch out for pests and diseases, and sit back and simply admire the product.

Climbers and ramblers
'Albertine' A glorious and popular rose for walls, tall hedges or screens. Its red-tinged foliage and stems make a good foil to the large, coppery-pink flowers with a lovely, cool, perfume. The long flowering season can be marred by bad weather.

R. brunonii **'La Mortola'** A vigorous climber with grey–green leaves, pink early on and masses of white or creamy flowers with a heavy fragrance that will fill the garden. 'La Mortola' is wonderful on big pergolas, screens, or large walls. It is not for cold or exposed gardens.

'Cécile Brunner' The climbing form of 'Cécile Brunner' is vigorous and good for walls or pergolas. It has exquisite, pink, 'hybrid tea' shaped blooms, heavily perfumed. It flowers abundantly until late summer, then occasionally into autumn.

'Danse du Feu' A vigorous climber, good on north-facing walls. The flowers are fiery orange red, fading to a darker bluish red. Not for the faint hearted, it flowers all season, and is good on tall tripods or a pergola. Cool down with other paler colours.

'Félicité et Perpétue' A splendid rose for screens, walls or tall poles. It is strong growing but won't engulf you. For a long season, it is covered with very double, pale-pink flowers, exquisite in bud.

R. filipes **'Kiftsgate'** A grand large-scale

Top *Plant roses in well-prepared soil, to which has been added peat enriched with bonemeal. Budded roses should be planted so that the union between rootstock and scion is just below the final soil level.*
Above *Newly planted bush roses, such as hybrid teas, should be pruned back hard as indicated by the 'pruning marks'. Always cut to an outward-facing bud.*

plant for gable walls, 'Kiftsgate' will turn a ramshackle garage into a romantic pavilion. A single but astonishing season of vast clusters of single, cream, scented flowers is followed by small red hips.

'Gloire de Dijon' A vigorous and handsome climber, this flowers well on north walls, but even better in sun. Its large, very double flowers, in buff apricot, are heavily scented. It has a fairly long season. If the plant gets scrawny below, plant low-growing ground cover in front.

'Golden Showers' This fairly perpetual flowering rose is a good yellow for tripods, poles or walls. Elegant buds, open to semi-double flowers, nicely scented.

'Madame Alfred Carrière' A vigorous climber that does well in shade; even more flowers are produced in sun. It is almost perpetual flowering, very double, with a wonderful perfume, the very palest possible pink. It cuts well and is very grand.

'Mermaid' This is another fast climber good on north walls, but even better in the sun. Immense, rather floppy, single, soft-yellow flowers. It looks good against old stone walls or weatherboarding but swamps bungalows.

'New Dawn' Fully perpetual flowering, the first flush leaves a snowfall of silvery-pink petals. The flowers are well shaped. Wonderful for walls or fences, it makes a good background for other roses or shrubs.

'Paul's Scarlet Climber' This vigorous climber is good on walls or pergolas and bears clusters of dog-rose flowers in intense red, paler in the centre and scarcely perfumed. It is unfortunately vulnerable to mildew.

'Souvenir de la Malmaison' A moderately strong climber, 'Souvenir de la Malmaison' is excellent on pillars or walls and produces a midsummer and early autumn flush of flowers. An 'old' flower shape, fully double, soft, fleshy pink, paler after opening, with a luscious scent.

'Wedding Day' This is vigorous, but not overpowering, with good, glossy leaves, and thornless stems. Vast flower clusters, deep-creamy yellow in bud are much paler when open. Good for screens, it can also be threaded along wires to make a hedge.

'Zéphirine Drouhin' A wonderful, thornless climber, this is easily pruned. It is heavily perfumed, with fully double flowers of a gorgeous, rich pink. Flowers are produced almost all summer and into early autumn. It is good for pillars.

Shrub roses

'Ballerina' A good dense shrub, this sometimes grows quite low. It makes an excellent hedge. Its big clusters of small, single flowers are light pink, shading dramatically to a white centre with yellow stamens.

'Blanc Double de Coubert' This eventually makes a large shrub. It has good foliage and a long season of substantial double, white flowers with a powerful fruity fragrance. It is excellent for the shrub border, or for hedging.

'Buff Beauty' Makes a good medium-sized shrub, or is splendid against a wall. It has a succession of flower clusters, each flower double, marvellously fragrant and an attractive colour in between apricot and beige.

'Canary Bird' Looks like a species rose and is lovely in flower with arching branches of delicate leaflets, supporting handsome single flowers of bright yellow. Excellent for the wild garden, or big shrub border.

'Céleste' This is a strong and eventually large Alba shrub with grey–green leaves and abundant, single pink flowers, of perfect form and perfect scent. Plant as a specimen, or by a path or back door. It has been popular since the 18th century.

'Complicata' An odd name, for a rose bearing enormous and perfect single roses, in a perfectly simple pink, shading to paler at the centre. It has a short season, but nothing is more spectacular.

'Comte de Chambord' A vigorous but fairly small shrub with yellowy green leaves, sumptuous and heavily perfumed flowers, a tight mass of rich pink petals. It has a longer season than most old roses, so should suit everyone.

'Constance Spry' A modern hybrid, using one 'old' parent making a good, slightly floppy bush. Fine dark leaves, set off the splendid, fully double, strongly fragrant, flowers with rich, slightly sharp, pink petals. Good on low walls, or amongst shrubs.

'Empress Josephine' Familiar since Tudor times, this weak shrub (also known as 'Francofurtana') bears the most wonderful, very double, very heavily scented, flowers of a sumptuous bluish pink, shading to an intense centre.

'Felicia' A superb rose for any garden, either in the shrubbery, or as a dense hedge. It covers itself with flowers in midsummer, and with lots more later. They are buff-pink in bud, silvery pink after opening.

'Ispahan' One of *the* old roses and still used for making 'attar of roses'. The flowers are very double, of perfect form, gorgeously scented, intense pink, and appear over quite a long season. They cut well. Plant it by walls, steps, or against a dark background of foliage.

'Little White Pet' If you read the description of 'Félicité et Perpétue', but thought it might be too big for your garden,

Opposite 1 *For a spectacular rose hedge, try the old 'Rosa Mundi' with its unusual striped flowers.*
2 *The large-flowered bush rose 'Fragrant Cloud' is heavily perfumed but prone to the disease blackspot.*
3 *'Grandpa Dickson', also a large-flowered bush rose, is an excellent yellow but has very little fragrance.*
4 *'Whisky Mac' was one of the very first of the amber-coloured, large-flowered bush roses and is still popular.*
5 *The cluster-flowered bush rose 'Elizabeth of Glamis' is very vigorous but unfortunately is rather prone to diseases.*
6 *One of the finest white cluster-flowered bush roses, 'Iceberg' is excellent for bedding or mass planting and the flowers are good for cutting.*

grow this charming bush form of the climber. It looks lovely by doorways, or flopping over a low wall.

'Lord Penzance' An attractive, slightly gawky briar, with tiny jagged leaflets, which smell of apple pie, especially after rain. The briar-like flowers are abundant, rosy buff with yellow centres. Good in semi-wild gardens, or by paths in glossier, more formal ones.

'Madame Hardy' Makes a good strong bush, quite big if happy, with pale green leaves. The perfect white flowers have an intriguing green 'eye' and a wonderful cool, clear, smell. Very sophisticated – perfect with pale delphiniums, ferns, 'Bowles Mauve' wallflowers or pulmonarias.

R. moyesii **'Geranium'** A lanky shrub, tall if happy. Single flowers appear on each side shoot, in an astonishing red. Large vase-shaped hips of a different, but equally exciting shade follow. The hips last until winter. Plant near to a path.

'Nevada' Eventually makes a large shrub, so plant at the back of the border. Spectacular when the first flowering covers every branch with large single cream (sometimes with a pink flush) flowers with slight fragrance. Scattered flowers appear until autumn.

'Rosa Mundi' A medieval, if not older rose. Its pale green leaves are smothered for a few weeks with heavily perfumed, double flowers, striped in palest and deeper cerise pink. It makes a stunning hedge but clip over after flowering. Petals may be dried for pot-pourri.

'Roseraie de l'Hay' A stout, medium sized shrub, with handsome leaves and very handsome double flowers, rich velvety crimson-purple, with a heady perfume to match. A long season, though few hips follow. Excellent for hedging and splendid planted by a seat.

R. rubrifolia A splendid, moderately sized shrub with fine greyish-red foliage making a wonderful background to other plants. Small dog-rose flowers are followed by black hips. Not a showy plant, but beautiful.

Bush roses
Large flowered

'Alec's Red' A popular hybrid tea, with all of that group's attractive fragrance. An abundance of flowers, a good bright cherry red, with a good shape. Vigorous and a rose with few problems.

'Fragrant Cloud' Deservedly a most popular variety, the perfume living up to the name, and produced by fine coral scarlet flowers of excellent shape. They grow either singly, or in clusters. A vigorous plant, though watch for blackspot.

'Grandpa Dickson' These medium sized plants, have enormous, rather open flowers of lemon yellow, fading rather paler and often with pink edges to the petals. All too luscious for some, but other gardeners love them despite their poor fragrance.

'Just Joey' Good strong bushes, supporting coppery orange flowers, the slightly frilled petals dramatically threaded with red veins.

'Silver Jubilee' A strong growing, disease resistant bush with attractive glossy foliage. The flowers are large and handsome, lusciously coloured in pink, but shaded with oranges and cream.

'Whisky Mac' This nice bush is fairly compact and vigorous. The flowers are attractively shaped and full of petals, fragrant but not intoxicating. Their shade of amber is close to some sorts of the drink.

Cluster flowered

'Allgold' A good bush, or a shrub if you leave it alone when it will flower early, too. The handsome flowers of a good deep yellow are not in the least harsh. They cut well and are of moderate fragrance.

'Café' The dark foliage (watch out for mildew) makes a fine setting for the fully double flowers, flattish when finally open, in a pretty series of coffee shades.

'Elizabeth of Glamis' An attractive, vigorous and popular plant. The fine and full flowers are of a slightly orange pink, smell good and cut well.

'Glenfiddich' A vigorous and healthy bush. The flowers are of quite good shape, and a nice peaty yellow that works well with all the other yellows in the group.

'Iceberg' A bedding rose, or a bush if you don't prune, with nice glossy leaves and loose sprays of the hybrid tea shaped flowers of perfect white. The flowers cut beautifully, and look good by candlelight.

'Korresia' A floribunda with dusky golden yellow flowers of perfect shape, it is a strong grower, and generally quite healthy.

'Lavender Lassie' Makes a tall graceful shrub if left unpruned with clusters of double, rather flattened flowers in a pale pinkish lilac. An excellent rose.

'Margaret Merrill' An attractive bush, the flowers open to a warmer white than 'Iceberg', and so are preferred by many; (the buds are pink). It has a good fragrance and blends well with pink and red roses.

Miniatures

'Cinderella' This is a real miniature less than 30cm (12in) high, with the tiniest of white roses, rosette shaped, with a slightly pinkish centre. It is very graceful.

'Perle de Montserrat' A tiny pink rose, with petals that are darker on the reverse and so have an interesting effect. Best planted where it's easily seen.

INDEX

Picture Credits

Front cover: Harry Smith Horticultural Photographic Collection

Back cover: Marshall Cavendish Library

Heather Angel: 32(tr); D. Arminson: 17; P. Becker: 31(tr,bl); K. Beckett: 39(tl), 55(tr), 57(bl); R. J. Corbin: 32(br), 66(t,b), 67(t); J. Cowley: 14(tl), 55(bl), 61(bl); Ernest Crowson: 69(cl,cr,bl,br), 71(tr); Alan Duns: 39(tr), 43(cl), 49(tl), 51(cl), 57(tl,cl); Ray Duns: 14(bl), 16; Valerie Finnis: 49(tr), 63(tl); P. Genereux: 37(bl), 43(bl), 51(cr); J. Howden: 33(bl); P. Hunt: 43(br), 55(cr), 63(cr), 69(tl); A. J. Huxley: 18(r), 43(tr); George Hyde: 30(bl), 30/1, 31(br), 37(tr), 63(bl); ICI: 29; Leslie Johns: 37(br); John Ledger: 19; J. Markham: opposite title page; P. Mathews: 69(tr), 71(tl,cl,cr,bl,br); Elsa Megson: 45(bl); Murphy Chemical Co.: 33(cr,br); M. Newton: 37(cr), 43(cr), 63(cl); M. Nimmo: 57(cr); S. J. Orme: 51(bl); C. Reynolds: 18(l); Royal Horticultural Society, Wisley: 30(tl); I. Ruthven: 7; A. Schilling: 32(bl); Shell: 32(tl), 33(t); Miki Slingsby: 37(tl), 61(cl); Harry Smith Horticultural Photographic Collection: 15, 37(cl), 45(cr), 49(cr,br), 51(br), 55(cl), 57(tr,br), 61(tr), 63(tr); Colin Watmough: 39(br), 43(tl), 51(tr), 63(br); D. Wildridge: 61(cr,br).